ENDORSEMENTS

These inspiring stories recount God's miraculous intervention in Dr. and Mrs. Gills' daily lives. Each incident offers an excellent example of God's love, abundant provision, and perfect timing. As you read and reread *Miracles Are Still Happening,* you will be encouraged to stand firm on your faith and believe God for your miracle!

— *Joyce Meyer*

We read *Miracles Are Still Happening,* and we think it is absolutely incredible! There is nothing in the world that will build people's faith faster than listening to miracles that happened to somebody else. As much as we love miracles, and as much as we walk in them, nevertheless, every story that they told boosted our faith once again.

We especially liked the way they started each chapter with personal miracles of their own. They have done an excellent job in writing, and we think this is a fantastic book.

— *Charles and Frances Hunter*

Miracles Are Still Happening

Miracles Are Still Happening

A.L. & Joyce Gill

Whitaker House

MIRACLES ARE STILL HAPPENING

Gill Ministries
P. O. Box 99
Fawnskin, CA 92333
E-mail: algill@bigbear.net

ISBN: 0-88368-620-1
Printed in the United States of America
Copyright © 2000 by A.L. and Joyce Gill

Whitaker House
30 Hunt Valley Circle
New Kensington, PA 15068

Library of Congress Cataloging-in-Publication Data

Gill, A. L.
    Miracles are still happening / by A.L. and Joyce Gill.
        p. cm.
    ISBN 0-88368-620-1 (pbk.)
    1. Miracles. 2. Christian life. 3. Gill, A. L. 4. Gill, Joyce. I.
Gill, Joyce. II. Title.
BT97.2 .G55 2000
231.7'3—dc21   00-009596

1 2 3 4 5 6 7 8 9 10 11 12 / 09 08 07 06 05 04 03 02 01 00

TABLE OF CONTENTS

Foreword

Thousands of miracles along Galilee, flowing from the touch of Jesus, heralded the birth of Christianity. Was this awesome display of God's power to be just a one-time phenomena?

During Jesus' final days on earth, He said to us, "I give you power over all the power of the enemy" and, "Greater things shall you do than Me, as I go to be with the Father." The small company of His disciples and apostles then went forth with miracles and wonders bursting in their footsteps, and "turned the world upside down."

Dr. A.L. and Joyce Gill's book highlights the truth that God continues to use miracles to show His love and to help ignite revival fires. His presence and His power must now be acted upon by each of us to bring in this last great harvest of lost souls.

A.L. and Joyce Gill, through their international broadcasts, books, and travel, have deeply affected the regions where more than a billion souls are benefited.

Miracles Are Still Happening is truly a must read!

— *George Otis*

A Note to the Reader

Throughout this book, specific biblical miracles are mentioned. Many of these miracles are not referenced within the text so that the flow of thought will not be interrupted. Scripture references to each miracle cited are included in the final section of the book and are listed in chronological order, as they are mentioned in the book, for easy reference.

What If...?

What if...

God's Word is true?

What if...

Jesus temporarily laid aside His divine rights and privileges when He came to this earth in the form of a man – the Last Adam – and that all His healings and miracles were accomplished through the power of the Holy Spirit?

What if...

Jesus meant it when He said that the works that He did we shall do also, and greater works than these we shall do?

What if...

When Jesus left this earth, He sent the Holy Spirit to empower us to do the same miracles that He did?

What if...

The miracles recorded in the Old Testament, in the life of Jesus, and in the book of Acts, could actually happen in our lives today?

This can be the beginning of an exciting, awesome, powerful, new way of living. We can begin to live in the supernatural realm of the Spirit. From this day forward, we can experience miracles happening in our lives!

For this to occur, we need to go back and look at the Word of God again, not as theologians or historians, but as those who will, with simplicity of faith, believe God's Word is true.

Let's look again at what the Word of God says we can do, how we can live, function, and minister in today's world. Jesus said, I am the vine, you are the branches. He who abides in Me, and I in him, bears much fruit; for without Me you can do nothing (John 15:5).

— A.L. and Joyce Gill

When all the people were baptized, it came to pass that Jesus also was baptized; and while He prayed, the heaven was opened. And the Holy Spirit descended in bodily form like a dove upon Him, and a voice came from heaven which said, "You are My beloved Son; in You I am well pleased."...Then Jesus returned in the power of the Spirit to Galilee.
—Luke 3:21–22; 4:14

Most assuredly, I say to you, he who believes in Me, the works that I do he will do also; and greater works than these he will do, because I go to My Father.
—John 14:12

But you shall receive power when the Holy Spirit has come upon you; and you shall be witnesses to Me in Jerusalem, and in all Judea and Samaria, and to the end of the earth.
—Acts 1:8

Heal the sick, cleanse the lepers, raise the dead, cast out demons. Freely you have received, freely give.
—Matthew 10:8

CHAPTER ONE

Miracles, Miracles, Miracles

Our Lives Were Changed

"Get A.L. out of town while he's still alive!" These words from A.L.'s doctor gripped my heart with fear and desperation. Was my husband going to die at the age of thirty-three? Would I be left alone to raise our two children?

It was 1968, and our lives had turned from believing in the American Dream to ones of desperation. Financially, we could see no way out, and now A.L.'s health was gone. Where had we gone wrong? We had both asked Jesus into our hearts when we were young children. We had gone to Bible school. We were active in our church. We were trying to serve the Lord, but with these appalling words, all hope was gone.

Little did we know we were about to step into a whole new way of living. We were about to step from the natural to the supernatural realm.

We took the doctor's words literally, and soon our family piled into our small sedan and started the drive from Houston, Texas, to Los Angeles, California.

A.L. was unable to drive, and hour after hour, I was at the wheel. I was desperate, and there was one thought in my mind — Get out of town for A.L.'s sake, before it's too late for him.

In New Mexico, I was driving on a four-lane divided high-way, and the terrain between the east and west lanes was steep and rough. It was late. I was tired, but was still rushing to make it to the next town. Driving at about seventy miles an hour, I pulled into the left lane to pass a large eighteen-wheeler. Just when our car was parallel to the truck, it also started pulling into the left lane. I hit the brakes as hard as I could, but there was no way to get back behind the truck. Its wheels were getting closer and closer as I pulled more and more to the left. Finally — seconds seemed like minutes — I was forced to leave the highway and take the car down the rough, steep embankment between the two roads.

We had seen a car earlier that day that had rolled in the same type of area, and I knew we were in trouble. The steering wheel jerked this way and that, and it took all my strength to hold the car in a straight path. There were two concrete poles ahead. I couldn't drive around them, and so I tried to aim the car between them, even as I realized there wasn't enough width for the car. I felt the rear wheels start to slide out of control. "God help us!" I cried out.

Instantly, our car was stopped!

None of us had any impression of stopping. We weren't thrown forward. We were just...stopped. When I cried out, I felt a large, warm, comforting hand take control of the steering wheel and the car. It was still there, resting over my right hand. I could feel it, but I couldn't see it. The two concrete poles were still ahead. A.L. had put his hands out, ready to grab the steering wheel if I tried to jerk the car back to the right, and his hands were still there about six inches from the wheel. Everything was frozen in time while my mind tried to comprehend what had just happened.

There was no understanding it. We had moved from the natural to the supernatural realm. From that day forward, our lives would never be the same.

*D*id our personal miracle mean God still works miracles today? we wondered. We had been told miracles had ceased, but was that true? We began to search the Word, and we found the Bible to be a book of miracles. From Genesis to Revelation, it's a recording of the supernatural. And yet, many of us have studied it as the history of what God did with the children of Israel, what God did when Jesus walked on this earth, and what God did when the apostles were alive. We have failed to understand it as a record of how God miraculously works with His people even to this present time.

Creation Is a Miracle

God created the earth – a miracle. He created everything in the sea, on the earth, even Adam and Eve – all miracles.

Job couldn't explain creation. He wrote, **God thunders marvelously with His voice; He does great things which we cannot comprehend (Job 37:5).**

Many years ago, I decided to read through the Bible and underline every miracle I found. I opened my Bible to the first words in Genesis, **In the beginning God created the heavens and the earth...,** and I began laughing at myself. The Bible is a record of miracles from the beginning to the end. I had just been reading it with my natural mind.

The Bible Is a Miracle

The very existence of the Bible is also a miracle. Jesus promised, **For assuredly, I say to you, till heaven and earth pass away, one jot or one tittle will by no means pass from the law till all is fulfilled (Matthew 5:18).**

The Bible has been hated by various people through the ages. Copies have been collected and burned in one era after another. Believers have been forbidden to possess it or to read it. They have died for having just a small part of it in their possession. And yet, in 1947, when the scrolls were discovered in the Judean desert near the Dead Sea, whole sections of the Scriptures were found among the ancient manuscripts, documents that are word for word as the Hebrew Bible is today. Over a period of almost ten years, thousands of scroll fragments were found in eleven different caves, but no serious discrepancies were discovered when they were compared with other Old Testament manuscripts. God has miraculously protected and preserved His Word.

The Bible is a miracle in its existence – antiquity – accuracy – harmony – preservation – preparation – and in its abiding power. This is important to us, because everything we believe, say, or do should be based solidly on what God has written in His Word.

What Is a Miracle?

When we say something is a miracle, what do we mean? A miracle is any event that appears unexplainable by the laws of nature, and so it is held to be supernatural in origin. A miracle interrupts the natural flow of things. Sometimes a miracle defies the laws of nature.

Miracles in the Old Testament

Let's look at some of the miracles in the Old Testament. There is the miracle of God's judgment on the ancient world and Noah's supernatural protection (and through him, the safeguarding of the future of the human race) during the flood. This miracle of protection is a picture of believers being protected from the judgment of God.

The miracle of Sarah's womb coming back to life and her conceiving Isaac is a picture of the new birth, of the dead being reborn.

We read about the miracle of Enoch's translation. Enoch walked with God; and he was not, for God took him (Genesis 5:24). This is a picture of believers being caught up to meet Jesus in the air.

What about Moses? Were there miracles in his life? God preserved his life using a small basket floating on the river Nile. And this was just the first of many miracles God did to set His people free. God came to Moses in the burning bush. Following that, there are the miracles of Moses' rod turning into a snake – the plagues in Egypt – the parting of the Red Sea – supernatural water – supernatural manna and supernatural quail – clothing and shoes that didn't wear out – the supernatural cloud giving shade in the desert by day and giving warmth at night by changing to fire – the Ten Commandments written by the finger of God. The list goes on and on, and we can only begin to fathom the greatness of God through the miracles He has worked for His people.

When we remember that the children of Israel are a type, or picture, of believers today, we can begin to understand how God deals with His people and how He desires to work miracles in our time.

In the book of Joshua, we find more supernatural events in the parting of the Jordan River – the Commander of the Lord's army appearing to Joshua – hail destroying the armies at Gibeon – the sun standing still – and the walls of Jericho falling flat.

In Judges, we read about Gideon putting out the fleece and the miracles during Samson's life and death. In 1 Samuel, we find Dagon falling on his face before the ark of God.

And how could we forget the miraculous stories of David defeating Goliath, of Jonah and the whale, of Hezekiah being healed, and even of God letting the shadow of the sun go back ten degrees to confirm that healing?

The Old Testament is full of miracles. Miraculous events happened in the lives of judges and kings, of common people, and of the prophets.

Miracles and the Prophets

When we look at the life of Elijah, we are astounded at the miracles that happened. He stopped and started the rain – was fed first by ravens and then through the multiplication of oil and flour. He brought the widow's son back to life – had fire fall from heaven – divided the Jordan River in order to walk across it – and was translated into heaven in a chariot of fire.

Elisha asked for a double portion of Elijah's anointing, and there are exactly twice as many miracles recorded in his life as in Elijah's. Immediately after Elijah's death, Elisha also parted the Jordan River and walked across. He multiplied oil for the widow and her sons. He prophesied the birth of the Shunammite's son, and then, years later, when the boy died, brought him back to life. He made the poisoned pottage good to eat. He made the iron ax head float. He healed Naaman of leprosy and put that same leprosy on his servant Gehazi because of his sin. He opened blind eyes, and after he died, even his bones brought life to a dead man.

What God Did Before, He Will Do Again

The Bible is a recording of the miraculous! It's impossible to believe the Bible and not believe in miracles. Over and over, through the Old Testament, we find events that cannot be explained by the natural mind – events that must be accepted by faith. To be true believers in God, to truly believe His Word is true, we must believe that supernatural events really happened. Our God is a God of miracles.

24

In Malachi, we read, For I am the LORD, I do not change (Malachi 3:6). In Hebrews, we find, Jesus Christ is the same yesterday, today, and forever (Hebrews 13:8).

What God did for the children of Israel, He will do for us. What He did for the prophets, He will do for us. What He did for Abraham, Moses, Joshua, Samuel, and all the rest, He will do for us!

CHAPTER TWO

Jesus Performed Miracles

Jesus Performed Miracles

The Traffic I Couldn't See

It was A.L. who was dying, but I was certainly involved. When I tried to sleep at night, I could feel my muscles snapping against the mattress. Physically, I was as tense as the strings on a violin. We were "borrowing from Peter to pay Paul" every payday. Because of the interest on our credit cards, our debts were growing continuously. We had come to the end financially, A.L. had come to the end physically, and I had come to the end emotionally. With-out A.L., I didn't want to go on living.

Where was God? We had believed in Him for almost all our lives, but where was He?

When God stopped our car and saved us from serious injury or even death, it was as though He made a dramatic entrance into our lives. He came off the pages of our Bibles and into our arena. Our belief in Him moved from our natural minds to our spirits. He was real! He was with us! You would think we would have been so thankful that nothing would ever again have bothered us and we'd never have had another problem, but that wasn't the way it was.

The day after God supernaturally stopped our car, I was driving into Los Angeles during the evening rush-hour traffic.

There were cars everywhere, and traffic was moving at seventy miles an hour. I didn't know the freeways at all. I had been driving in this traffic for over an hour, and a frenzy was building inside of me.

As I was making a transition between two freeways, I was on one of those slow, twenty-mile-per-hour curves. I knew our car wouldn't be able to accelerate to seventy miles an hour and merge with traffic on the new freeway. And I needed to cross immediately all the way to the left lane for the next exit. It was an impossibility! And right there, in the middle of that curve, everything snapped. Tears were running down my face, and I started saying, "I can't make it! I can't go on!" I meant the traffic, but also my life...but there was no way to stop. There was no way to get off.

As our car came to the top of the curve, I looked through my tears for an opening onto the freeway, and it was completely open! I drove across several lanes, from the right side of the freeway to the left, and there wasn't a vehicle in sight. It was as though we had the freeway to ourselves. We looked around. Were we on a closed freeway? And then, suddenly, traffic was all around us, beside us, in front of us, behind us, everywhere.

I don't know what happened. I think God blinded my eyes to the traffic and took us safely through. And then when I was in the left lane ready for the next exit, He let me see the traffic again.

But now, in my innermost being, I knew God was in control! When He stopped our car, it wasn't a one-time, supernatural intervention of God. There was more of Him to be found.

*W*hen we look at the miracles of Jesus, it's as though Jesus was all the prophets, all the judges, and all the kings rolled into one Person. The miracles in the Old Testament happened over a period of four thousand years. Jesus had only three and a half years of ministry, and He moved in the miraculous every day of that time. He healed the sick; He set the captives free; He loosed those whom Satan had bound. However, before we get into a discussion of the miracles Jesus performed, we should consider the miracles surrounding His birth, especially the appearances of angels and the giving of divine guidance through dreams.

Miracles Surrounding Christ's Birth

An angel appeared to Mary and said, Do not be afraid, Mary, for you have found favor with God. And behold, you will conceive in your womb and bring forth a Son, and shall call His name JESUS (Luke 1:30–31).

And an angel appeared to Joseph in a dream saying, Joseph, son of David, do not be afraid to take to you Mary your wife, for that which is conceived in her is of the Holy Spirit (Matthew 1:20).

The third angelic visit surrounding the birth of Jesus involved one angel and then many more angels who appeared to the shepherds to announce Jesus' birth. It's as though the angels were so excited about what was happening that they burst from the realm of the Spirit into the natural realm of mankind.

The wise men followed the star that appeared in the East, and they came to Jesus; then were warned by God in a supernatural dream that they were not to return to Herod, but instead to go home another way.

There was another miraculous dream, and an angel appeared to Joseph and warned him to take Jesus and Mary to Egypt. The angel went on to tell him of Herod's plan to kill Jesus and that they were to remain in Egypt until he, the angel, came back to tell them it was safe to return.

The books of Matthew, Mark, and Luke all start with miraculous events surrounding the birth of Jesus. There are three hundred and thirty messianic prophecies in the Old Testament that are fulfilled in Jesus' birth, life, and death.

Jesus' Miracles of Healing

But what about the miracles Jesus did? Of course, immediately, healing comes to mind. The second miracle Jesus did was to heal the nobleman's son. Remember how Jesus said, "Go your way, your son lives," and then the servants came confirming that the nobleman's son was healed at that very same time?

There was the leper who asked, "If You're willing..." And Jesus immediately answered, "I'm willing, be clean."

There was the paralytic who was lowered through the roof by his friends. And when Jesus saw their faith, He said to the sick man, "Arise, take up your bed, and go to your house."

There was the man at the Pool of Bethesda. Remember how an angel would come down and stir the water, and the first one in would be healed? With all the people waiting for the water to be stirred, Jesus went to this one man and asked, "Would you be made whole?" This man had been sick for thirty-eight years, and Jesus said, "Arise, take up your bed and walk," and the man was instantly healed.

Another man with a withered hand was in the synagogue. To him, Jesus said, "Stretch forth your hand," and his hand was completely restored.

There was the woman with an issue of blood who pushed through the crowd and touched the hem of Jesus' garment and was instantly made well.

We could go on and on telling of the miracles of healing that are recorded. In Matthew, Jesus healed a man who was possessed with a demon, and who was blind and mute. There were two blind men who called out, "Have mercy on us," and were healed. Another blind man was healed at Bethsaida when Jesus spit on his eyes and laid hands on him. The man who was born blind was healed in Jerusalem. And Bartimaeus, the blind beggar, was healed at Jericho.

There are the healings of the centurion's servant, the Syrophoenician woman's daughter, the ten lepers, the man with dropsy; and even at the end, when the officers and soldiers came from the chief priests and elders to arrest Jesus, He healed the servant of the high priest after Peter cut off his ear.

There are over twenty incidents of healing told in various details in the Gospels. But that was still just a beginning of healing miracles, because we read, over and over, how "Jesus healed them all," how "He healed every one of them," that "as many as touched the hem of His garment were healed," how "power went out from Him and healed them all."

Actually, Matthew said it best, Great multitudes came to Him, having with them the lame, blind, mute, maimed, and many others; and they laid them down at Jesus' feet, and He healed them. So the multitude marveled when they saw the mute speaking, the maimed made whole, the lame walking, and the blind seeing; and they glorified the God of Israel (Matthew 15:30–31).

The Gospels are full of healing miracles! But the miracles of Jesus didn't stop with the healings of the multitudes we read about. There were other kinds of miracles, too.

Jesus' Miracles of Deliverance

Jesus set the captives free. He cast the unclean spirit out of the demoniac in the synagogue at Capernaum. He cast the demons out of the man at Gadarene and allowed them to go into the herd of swine. He cast the spirit of infirmity out of the woman who had been bent over for eighteen years.

Jesus' Miracles over Nature

Jesus performed miracles that showed His authority over nature. The first miracle was changing water into wine at the marriage feast in Cana. He fed the multitudes twice. The first time, it was a crowd of over five thousand men plus unnumbered women and children, which He fed with five loaves and two fish. The second time, it was a crowd of over four thousand men, again with unnumbered women and children, and He multiplied seven loaves and a few fish for them all to be fed.

Two times there were miraculous amounts of fish caught when Jesus' instructions were followed. And there was the single fish that Peter caught with the tax money in its mouth.

He spoke to the storm, "Peace, be still!" and it was. He cursed the fig tree for not bearing fruit, and it died. He walked on the water.

Jesus' Miracles of Raising the Dead

When Jarius' daughter died, Jesus raised her from the dead. He raised the widow of Nain's son from the dead during the funeral procession. He raised Lazarus from the dead after he had been dead for four days!

Jesus Still Does Miracles Today

Jesus operated in the supernatural realm throughout His entire ministry. Miracles happened everywhere He went, and miracles still happen through Him today.

Doing the Works of Jesus!

CHAPTER THREE

Doing the Works of Jesus!

I Tell You, I'm Healed!

We had experienced miracles on the highway, but A.L.'s health was still gone. Our lives were still at an end. During two days of driving across country, I kept hearing the words, "You have not because you ask not!" I couldn't get away from them. Over and over, they kept repeating.

Hadn't we asked the Lord to give the doctors wisdom? Hadn't we asked the Lord to show us what to do for A.L.'s health? What hadn't we asked? The gifts of healings had ceased, hadn't they?

As A.L. and I discussed these words and our questions, neither of us realized that God was speaking to us. In the church of our tradition, we were told that the only way you could hear from God was to read His Word. And yet, now that we had experienced the supernatural, we were ready to believe there was more than what we knew.

Finally, we realized the only thing we hadn't asked God for was A.L.'s healing.

That evening in Los Angeles, there were six adults in the room — my sister, her family, and A.L.'s parents. All of us believed in God, but until this time, none of us had prayed for healing. We hadn't seen anyone else pray for healing. We didn't know how to pray for anyone to be healed!

Someone suggested it might be good if we each took a promise out of a Bible promise box. When we read them out loud, we realized all six promises had to do with healing.

We joined hands, and that seemed awkward because we had never prayed that way before. A.L. turned to his father and said, "Dad, you're the head of the family. Why don't you pray?" Dad cleared his throat a few times, and then he began by using the verses we had just read. "Father, Your Word says..." As he prayed God's Word, faith began to stir in our spirits. He finished by saying, "We're asking You now to heal A.L."

A.L. told us that while Dad prayed, he felt warmth flow all through his body. He had felt the touch of God! He knew he was healed, but the rest of us weren't so convinced. Several times that evening, A.L.'s mom or I told A.L. to lie back down before he passed out. We thought he was just psyching himself up.

I will never forget him lying on that blue couch with his head on a pillow to please us, and still declaring over and over, "I tell you, I am healed!"

Our prayer that evening wasn't a prayer of faith. It was more like a prayer of desperation. But God completely, totally, unconditionally, healed A.L., and that was over thirty years ago.

A.L. is walking in divine health. His ministry travels have taken him to over sixty nations of the world. Instead of my being left alone to raise two children, we now have three children and grandchildren. Instead of our life together being over, it had just begun.

What an awesome God we serve!

*M*ost assuredly, I say to you, he who believes in Me, the works that I do he will do also; and greater works than these he will do, because I go to My Father (John 14:12).

We have read these words of Jesus hundreds of times, but we must confess that, for years, we never truly believed them. Yes, we would reason, Jesus said these words, but He couldn't really have meant them — especially for us. After all, Jesus was the Son of God. He could do anything! He was all-powerful. He knew everything. He was God, and we're just normal men and women.

We did believe there were a few "super Christians," such as the apostle Paul, who could do some of the works of Jesus. We believed there might be a few "especially chosen ones" even in our generation, but certainly it would be prideful to even imagine that we could do the works of Jesus. And of course, there was never even a thought in our minds that we could do the greater works Jesus spoke of here.

We put these words of Jesus on a shelf in our hearts and marked them, "Not understood!" And we left them there year after year. We couldn't admit, even to ourselves, that we didn't believe them. And then the revelation of how Jesus actually operated on this earth began to come.

Jesus Lived on Earth as a Man

Jesus was born of a virgin as a human being. He was still truly God, but He temporarily gave up His rights as God and came to this earth as a man. He was true humanity, but still undiminished Deity.

The apostle Paul wrote, Let this mind be in you which was also in Christ Jesus, who, being in the form of God, did not consider it robbery to be equal with God, but made Himself of no reputation, taking the form of a bondservant, and coming in the likeness of men. And being found in appearance as a man, He humbled Himself and became obedient to the point of death, even the death of the cross (Philippians 2:5–8).

The apostle used the Greek word *kenoo*, which is translated "of no reputation." According to *Strong's Greek New Testament Dictionary, kenoo* means "to empty." It means "to make void, to deprive of force." When used here of Christ, it means that He laid aside His equality with God or that He emptied Himself of the form of God to take on human characteristics.

When Jesus came to this earth, He came as a man. He voluntarily laid aside His rights and privileges as God for a time. Everything He did while He lived and ministered on this earth, He did as a man, not as God.

Jesus Moved in the Power of the Spirit

No miracles were recorded in the life of Jesus in Matthew, Mark, Luke, or John until He was baptized in the Jordan River and the Holy Spirit came upon Him in the form of a dove.

In his gospel, Mark wrote, It came to pass in those days that Jesus came from Nazareth of Galilee, and was baptized by John in the Jordan. And immediately, coming up from the water, He saw the heavens parting and the Spirit descending upon Him like a dove (Mark 1:9–10).

It was immediately after the Holy Spirit came on Jesus when He was baptized in the Jordan River that miracles started happening.

Jesus came as the Last Adam. It is written, "The first man Adam became a living being." The last Adam became a life-giving spirit (1 Corinthians 15:45).

Everything the first Adam was originally created to do, Jesus actually did. God had said of man, Let them have dominion... (Genesis 1:26). Jesus took dominion over demons, over living things, over the elements. Jesus walked on this earth in the authority and power God had originally given to mankind.

Why is this important to us? Why is it necessary that we understand that Jesus operated on this earth as a man – as a perfect man – as Adam was created to be? Because then, He is truly our example. We can understand how we can do the same works He did. His words can become alive in us!

Greater Works

Jesus said, The Spirit of the LORD is upon Me, because He has anointed Me to preach the gospel to the poor; He has sent Me to heal the brokenhearted, to proclaim liberty to the captives and recovery of sight to the blind, to set at liberty those who are oppressed; to proclaim the acceptable year of the LORD (Luke 4:18–19).

Jesus was talking to the disciples when He said, "Abide in Me, and I in you. As the branch cannot bear fruit of itself, unless it abides in the vine, neither can you, unless you abide in Me. I am the vine, you are the branches. He who abides in Me, and I in him, bears much fruit; for without Me you can do nothing (John 15:4–5). As we walk through life abiding in Jesus and allowing Him to abide in us, we will bear fruit.

How exciting it is to read the Gospels, the New Testament, the whole Bible, looking for the supernatural, looking for the miracles that are recorded. And when we read each one, we can stop and say, "I can do that! I can do that miracle! In the name of Jesus, I can do it too!"

Even when we accept the fact that we can do the works of Jesus, most of us stumble at the idea of doing greater works. Perhaps that's because we have limited our understanding to thinking *greater* means "stronger than" or "more important." *Greater* can also mean "larger in quantity or number."

More Works

The Greek word *meizon,* translated "greater" in John 14:12, could also be translated "more." Doing more works than Jesus would be easier to understand. Jesus had three and a half years to minister, and He was one person. Believers have had around two thousand years since Jesus walked on this earth, and they number in the millions.

Jesus never traveled more than a hundred miles from Jerusalem, but believers have encompassed the entire world. "Greater works" can mean "greater in time, greater in distance, and greater in number."

No longer are the works of Jesus limited to one man. They are happening around the world through the hands of millions of believers.

Multiplied Works

There is also the principle of multiplication. In Leviticus, we read, **Five of you shall chase a hundred, and a hundred of you shall put ten thousand to flight (Leviticus 26:8).** The writer of Deuteronomy said that one can put a thousand to flight and two can put ten thousand to flight when the Lord is involved (Deuteronomy 32:30).

The Power of Corporate Faith

The word *greater* could also refer to the strength of many people believing in unity, the strength of corporate faith. Jesus referred to this when He said, **Again I say to you that if two of you agree on earth concerning anything that they ask, it will be done for them by My Father in heaven (Matthew 18:19).**

We have many examples of corporate faith today. When thousands come to great healing crusades with the expectation of being healed – actively believing and moving in faith – thousands are healed. When one person gets out of a wheelchair, it helps other people in wheelchairs have faith, and many more are healed. One day in Columbia, South America, A.L. saw a hundred people get out of wheelchairs all in a matter of minutes, and an untold number of people dropped their crutches and took off their braces. In Brazil, a lady who went back to the arena to take care of some closing business the day after a healing crusade said she was awestruck when she saw a huge pile of wheelchairs, crutches, and braces in the center of the arena where they had been piled by the clean-up crew.

When we add our faith to the faith of others, we are truly operating as the body of Christ, and there is a powerful level of faith in which countless miracles can happen.

Different Works

Another interpretation of *greater* is "different." If Jesus and the disciples were riding on a bus or an airplane today, and Satan tried to cause an accident taking their lives, what would Jesus do? Would He allow the accident to take all their lives, or would He do a different work than He did in the time He walked on this earth?

The apostle John wrote, **And truly Jesus did many other signs in the presence of His disciples, which are not written in this book; but these are written that you may believe that Jesus is the Christ, the Son of God, and that believing you may have life in His name (John 20:30–31).**

We have two examples of "different" works in the book of Acts. About Peter, we learn, **Multitudes of both men and women...brought the sick out into the streets and laid them on** beds and couches, that at least the shadow of Peter passing by might fall on some of them. Also a multitude gathered from the surrounding cities to Jerusalem, bringing sick people and those who were tormented by unclean spirits, and they were all healed (Acts 5:14–16).

And we read about Paul, Now God worked unusual miracles by the hands of Paul, so that even handkerchiefs or aprons were brought from his body to the sick, and the diseases left them and the evil spirits went out of them (Acts 19:11–12).

We have no recorded incidents of cloths being taken from Jesus for healing or of Jesus' shadow bringing healing. They may have happened, but Matthew, Mark, Luke, and John didn't write about them.

Jesus has commissioned us to do the works that He did, and even greater works. He has given us the responsibility of doing the works that He did. And today, God is raising up an army of mighty believers ready to step out in faith and do these works.

CHAPTER FOUR

The Dunamis Power

The Dunamis Power

Don't Let It Be Speaking in Tongues!

A.L. *previously had not been able to work more than a few hours at a time. But God supernaturally moved us into a new position managing a Christian bookstore in California, and within two weeks of receiving his new health, A.L. was working twelve to fourteen hours a day.*

Soon we noticed that there were certain people we were drawn to – people who seemed to have a special relationship to God – people we would ask to pray about our various needs – people who had a special joy about them. We began to do a little detective work. It wasn't the churches they went to. They didn't seem to know each other. What was it? Finally, we got up our nerve and asked first one and then another, "Do you speak in tongues?" And they all answered yes.

"O God," we would pray, "we want all that you have for us, but please don't let it have anything to do with speaking in tongues. You've given us our job, our church, and our friends. Surely you don't want us to give all this up."

We worked for a Christian company – a non-charismatic company. A.L. was teaching the adult Sunday school class in our church, a non-charismatic church. Our friends were non-charismatic. Our families were non-charismatic. We could be as on fire for God as we wanted, but if we were to speak in tongues, we would lose our jobs, our church, and our friends, and the relationships in our family would certainly be strained. "God, You know it wouldn't do!" we would say. But the hunger for more of God grew and grew.

Some friends had received the baptism in the Holy Spirit, and they were going to be speaking at a church in Orange County one Sunday. We agreed to meet them there and have dinner with them after the service.

As they gave their testimonies, our spirits were saying, "Yes, that's the way we're feeling. That's our prayer." But our minds were saying, "Don't cross the line. You'll lose everything." They gave an invitation for those who would like to receive the filling of the Holy Spirit, and hundreds went forward. We didn't! But since we were going to eat with our friends later, we waited for them outside the prayer room.

A.L. was curious, and several times he looked into the room expecting to see something wild and out-of-order going on. "Everything seems to be in order," he would report when he came back.

Finally, we looked up and one of our friends was running toward A.L. "Everyone I've laid my hands on tonight has received the baptism in the Holy Spirit. Are you ready?" she asked.

A.L. was known for his diplomacy, and I was wondering how he was going to get out of this situation. But, he raised his hands and said, "Zap me!"

She put her hands on both sides of his face and said, "Jesus, baptize my brother in your Holy Spirit." A.L. fell back a few inches against the wall with his eyes closed, and he began to speak softly, like a foreigner. He was speaking whole sentences and paragraphs.

What's happening? I asked myself. It's like I don't even know this man!

Our other friend came to me and asked, "Do you want to receive the baptism in the Holy Spirit?"

"I don't even know what you're talking about," I said. And I didn't. Nothing that was happening was like the stories we had heard. He put his hands on my head and prayed, and I felt a warmth, like warm water, move from my toes all the way up my body until I was immersed to my mouth — and two or three syllables came out.

Coming from our background, we had looked at the baptism in the Holy Spirit as limited to speaking in tongues. Until we received His presence and His power that night, we never knew there was more than that. We have written this incident from that point of view, but we soon found there was so much more!

Our friends told us that night, "From this time on, you will feel a love for God like you have never felt before. You will find yourselves drawn to His Word. You will have more love for people, and you will experience power in your life." And we did.

One day when Jesus was talking to the disciples, He said, Nevertheless I tell you the truth. It is to your advantage that I go away; for if I do not go away, the Helper will not come to you; but if I depart, I will send Him to you (John 16:7).

Take a moment to picture this day in your mind. The disciples loved Jesus. They lived with Jesus. They saw the miracles He did. They sat and listened to Him teach. And yet, now they heard Him say, "It's better for you that I go away."

How their minds must have fought with this! How could it be better for them? Everything within them must have demanded that Jesus stay.

And Jesus even said, "It's to your advantage that I go away; for if I don't go away, the Helper will not come to

you." It was better for them, and for us, that Jesus leave, because He would send the Holy Spirit. This was God's plan. Jesus could only be in one place at a time, but the Holy Spirit would be in believers all over the world.

Jesus Operated in the Power of the Spirit

We know that Jesus operated on this earth in the power of the Holy Spirit. In Matthew 4:1 and 12:28, we read, Then Jesus was led up by the Spirit, and, If I cast out demons by the Spirit of God.... In Luke 4:1, we find, Then Jesus, being filled with the Holy Spirit.... In Acts 1:2, we read, He, through the Holy Spirit.... And in Hebrews 9:14, we read how Christ through the eternal Spirit offered Himself....

After we read that Jesus was baptized and filled with the Holy Spirit, immediately we read, Then Jesus, being filled with the Holy Spirit, returned from the Jordan and was led by the Spirit into the wilderness (Luke 4:1). He didn't go there through His own knowledge; the Spirit led Him.

The gifts of the Holy Spirit flowed through Jesus. Remember He had laid aside all His rights and privileges as God. But when He was talking to the woman at the well, He still knew about her past. How did He know? Through the word of knowledge.

We know Jesus operated in the discerning of spirits because He called evil spirits by name: Deaf and dumb spirit, I command you, come out of him (Mark 9:25).

When the woman with the issue of blood pushed through the crowd and touched the hem of Jesus' garment, Jesus, immediately knowing in Himself that power had gone out of Him, turned around in the crowd and said, "Who touched My clothes?" (Mark 5:30).

Jesus did not know, as the Son of Man, who touched Him. He stopped and asked, "Who touched my clothes?"

But let's look at the first part of this verse, Knowing power had gone out of Him. The Greek word translated "power" is *dunamis*. It is the most expressive word for explosive power in the Greek language. It's the root word from which we take our English word *dynamite*.

The word *dunamis* was used several times in connection with the power in Jesus. It was also used in connection with the apostle Paul, who wrote, My speech and my preaching were not with persuasive words of human wisdom, but in demonstration of the Spirit and of power [*dunamis*] (1 Corinthians 2:4). The apostle Paul ministered in the same power as Jesus, in *dunamis* power, in the power of the Holy Spirit.

It's not hard to believe that Jesus operated in the power of the Holy Spirit. It's not even too hard to believe that the great apostle Paul operated in the same power. And, yes, we can even believe that the other apostles also operated in this same power. But what does that have to do with us today?

We Are to Operate in the Power of the Spirit

When Jesus was getting ready to leave this earth, He said, But you shall receive power [*dunamis*] when the Holy Spirit has come upon you (Acts 1:8).

The same word for power that was used in describing the healing power in Jesus and in Paul was used to describe what was going to happen to 120 believers in the Upper Room.

We find the word *dunamis* several more times after the Holy Spirit came on the Day of Pentecost. It was used in connection with the apostles. And with great power [*dunamis*] the apostles gave witness to the resurrection of the Lord Jesus (Acts 4:33).

It was used in connection with Stephen. And Stephen, full of faith and power [*dunamis*], did great wonders and signs among the people (Acts 6:8).

It was used by the apostle Paul: Now to Him who is able to do exceedingly abundantly above all that we ask or think, according to the power [*dunamis*] that works in us (Ephesians 3:20).

As Spirit-baptized believers, we have the same "dynamite" power in us that was in the early believers. Doesn't it make sense that if Jesus did miracles through the power of the Holy Spirit, that if the disciples did miracles through the power of the Holy Spirit, that if we have the same Holy Spirit, we can do the same miracles?

How Does the Holy Spirit Operate Today?

How does the Holy Spirit operate in the world today? The manifestations of the Holy Spirit are what we call the gifts of the Spirit. They are tongues, interpretation of tongues, prophecy, discerning of spirits, words of wisdom and knowledge, the gifts of faith and healings, and the working of miracles.

In studying the gifts of the Holy Spirit, many of us have looked at them as special gifts for special times. We haven't realized they are a way of life for us all the time. They are not just to operate on Sunday morning between the worship time and the announcements. In fact, that isn't the New Testament pattern.

One hot summer day, A.L. and I were getting ready to do a seminar on the *Supernatural Gifts of the Holy Spirit*. As we were praying together before the meetings, I suddenly saw the most beautiful Christmas tree you can imagine. It was at least two stories high and was in an impressive entranceway to a very prestigious home. A beautiful staircase curved down from the floor above. There were beautiful presents stacked in abundance under the tree, some wrapped and some open. It was as if I were standing in the doorway, with the joyful anticipation of a mother waiting for

the children to come running down the stairs to see the tree and open their gifts.

And then I heard the most sorrowful voice you can imagine. "My people are not opening their gifts," God said. I felt so much anguish that tears began to flow down my face.

We've been given so much. We've been given the presence, leading, and power of the Holy Spirit, plus the wonderful gifts of the Holy Spirit. And yet, how many times have we left these gifts sitting under the tree unopened?

How it grieves the Father that this is so! The gifts of the Holy Spirit are not for just a few believers. The gifts of the Holy Spirit are a way of life, for every believer, for every day.

How do we know what the will of the Father is in any situation? We hear or we see in the Spirit-realm through the supernatural gifts of the Holy Spirit. We hear from God through the revelation gifts of the discerning of spirits, the word of knowledge, and the word of wisdom.

And when we have heard from God, and we acknowledge we have heard from God, faith is released, and we move into the power gifts of the Holy Spirit. The gift of faith, the working of miracles, and the gifts of healings come.

There is another gift of the Holy Spirit that is so important but so maligned – the gift of speaking in tongues. Jesus said that speaking in tongues is a sign that will accompany those who believe. The apostle Paul wrote more about speaking in tongues than anyone else. When instructing the Corinthians believers on the proper use of spiritual gifts, he said that he spoke in tongues more than they did. I thank my God I speak with tongues more than you all... (I Corinthians 14:18).

Paul wrote thirteen books of the New Testament. That means the man who, according to his own words, spoke in tongues more than the rest, wrote almost one-half of the New Testament.

Paul also said, He who speaks in a tongue edifies himself (1 Corinthians 14:4). The Greek word for "edifies" is *oiko-domeo*, and means "to be a house builder, to construct, or to confirm." The person who speaks in tongues builds himself up in the Spirit.

Paul said tongues are a sign for unbelievers. Therefore tongues are for a sign, not to those who believe but to unbelievers (1 Corinthians 14:22). And he warned us, Therefore, brethren...do not forbid to speak with tongues (1 Corinthians 14:39).

In our own lives, we have found that speaking in tongues is the entranceway to the supernatural. It is the way we move ourselves from the natural to the supernatural, from the natural way of thinking to the Spirit.

When we hear from God, the gifts of faith, healings, and even the working of miracles become the normal things to do.

One time A.L. was overseas, and I was driving home alone late at night. As I had fastened my seat belt, I had asked the Lord for protection on the car and on me. And then I had prayed, as I usually do, "Lord, don't let me bring harm to any person or car." I had gone a few miles on my way and changed from one road to another. The new highway was wide. There was no traffic, and I quickly accelerated up to speed and pulled into the right lane to be ready for the next turn. The Lord spoke sharply, "Get out of this lane!" I jerked my car to the left, and immediately I passed a car stopped in the right lane. Its lights were off, and a man was changing the rear tire. In the natural, I never would have seen this man in time to avoid hitting him.

Through a word of wisdom, a horrible accident was prevented. I wasn't in a highly anointed, special meeting. I hadn't sung song after song of praise and worship, creating a super-anointed atmosphere. I was just driving home, but I had asked the Lord to be involved in that ordinary time of driving.

The Holy Spirit and His *dunamis* power are in us. He wants to manifest Himself through us at all times for our own protection, the protection of our families, and for others. The gifts of the Holy Spirit provide a whole new miraculous way of living for the Spirit-filled believer.

Even as Peter climbed out of his boat and walked on the water to Jesus, we are to step out of our "comfort zones" of natural living and walk on the supernatural water. We are to live in the Spirit, walk in the Spirit, and operate in all nine of His supernatural gifts in our daily lives.

CHAPTER FIVE

The Greatest Miracle of All

CHAPTER FIVE

The Greatest Miracle of All

A Supernatural Communion

A group of intern pastors and their wives were using our vacation home in the mountains, and they had asked A.L. to serve communion. As we drove to the house on the Friday after Thanksgiving, A.L. was praying about how the Lord would have him do this. He understood that we were each to break off a piece of bread and share it with at least three others, saying, "This is the body of Christ, which was broken for you."

There were over forty people in the room, and when the elements of the communion were brought out, we saw that they had prepared a small roll of bread about five inches in length and an inch and a half thick. But A.L. knew he had heard from God, so he continued with his instructions to break off a piece and share it with at least three others. We were all obedient but, seeing the size of the loaf, were all breaking off the smallest possible pieces that we could share. Soon we were all laughing and sharing very tiny pieces of bread.

We shared with this person and that person, and this person and that person came to share with us. Without thinking about it, we kept on sharing "the body of Christ" with one another for about forty-five minutes. Then another person came over to me with a piece of bread, and when I broke off a piece, I realized that the piece I now held in my hand was about one fourth the size of the original loaf.

What was happening? We all realized the same thing at about the same time, and an awesome silence filled the room. Each of us gazed at the bread in our hand. Where had it come from?

Still, with no one saying a word, we walked back to the table and started putting the remaining bread back on the silver tray. The tray couldn't hold it all, and soon pieces of bread were spilling across the table. We looked with amazement at the pile of leftover bread as we realized we had all shared with everyone else in the room. Again, Jesus had multiplied the bread as He had with the multitudes.

*O*ur miraculous communion was not the greatest miracle that can occur. Jesus performs the greatest miracle of all – from the time He walked on this earth to our day – when people are born-again!

Miracles Are Signs

Jesus said to them, "Fill the waterpots with water." And they filled them up to the brim. And He said to them, "Draw some out now, and take it to the master of the feast." And they took it. When the master of the feast had tasted the water that was made wine, and did not know where it came from (but the servants who had drawn the water knew), the master of the feast called the bridegroom. And he said to him, "Every man at the beginning sets out the good wine, and when the guests have well drunk, then the inferior. You have kept the good wine until now!" This beginning of signs Jesus did in Cana of Galilee, and manifested His glory; and His disciples believed in Him (John 2:7–11).

Have you ever wondered why the first miracle Jesus did was to turn water into wine? Was it that important to keep the host of the wedding feast from being embarrassed? To fully understand a truth in the Bible, we must go back to the first mention of that truth. So why is turning water into wine important to us? How does this miracle relate to every other miracle performed by Jesus?

Jesus took the natural element (water) and turned it into that which was supernatural (wine). John wrote that this miracle was the beginning of signs. But, what is a sign?

What Is a Sign?

Signs are miracles that bring revelation and communicate truth. Signs point to something beyond themselves. Signs are not to call attention to the people through whom they come, and they are not just for amazement. They are for the purpose of revealing truth.

The Miracle of the New Birth

When Jesus turned the water into wine, He gave us a visual picture of the new birth. Turning the water into wine was a sign pointing to the complete transformation of lives through the miracle of the new birth, a transformation from that which is natural to that which is of the Spirit.

In the third chapter of John, Jesus explained the new birth to Nicodemus, who was a ruler of the Jews. This man came to Jesus by night and said to Him, "Rabbi, we know that You are a teacher come from God; for no one can do these signs that You do unless God is with him."

Jesus answered and said to him, "Most assuredly, I say to you, unless one is born again, he cannot see the kingdom of God."

Nicodemus said to Him, "How can a man be born when he is old? Can he enter a second time into his mother's womb and be born?"

Jesus answered, "Most assuredly, I say to you, unless one is born of water and the Spirit, he cannot enter the kingdom of God. That which is born of the flesh is flesh, and that which is born of the Spirit is spirit. Do not marvel that I said to you, 'You must be born again'" (John 3:2–7).

Being born of the Spirit is the most important miracle in any person's life. Before we can experience being filled with the *dunamis* power of God, we must be born again. Only then can we enter into a new realm and experience the other miraculous provisions of God.

When we are born again, we become new creations. Therefore, if anyone is in Christ, he is a new creation; old things have passed away; behold, all things have become new (2 Corinthians 5:17).

What do we mean when we say people have been "saved," "converted," or have "accepted Jesus as their personal Savior"? Many of us are still back with Nicodemus. We're still pondering, "How can a person go through the birth process again?" But that's thinking in the natural! Jesus said that being born again is a birth of the Spirit.

Just as water being turned into wine is a picture of the new birth, it is also a picture of a person moving from the realm of the soul, or flesh, to realm of the Spirit, from the natural to the supernatural. Wine is a biblical symbol for the Holy Spirit.

Paul wrote, But you are not in the flesh but in the Spirit, if indeed the Spirit of God dwells in you. Now if anyone does not have the Spirit of Christ, he is not His (Romans 8:9).

He also wrote, Now we have received, not the spirit of the world, but the Spirit who is from God, that we might know the things that have been freely given to us by God....But the natural man does not receive the things of the Spirit of God, for they are foolishness to him; nor can he know them, because they are spiritually discerned (1 Corinthians 2:12, 14).

Salvation is beyond comprehension! That's why it can only be received by faith. In the natural, there is no understanding of the complete meaning of being born again. God is Spirit. We are created in His image. We are born of the Spirit, and we become His children. That means we are spirit too.

Paul referred to this as "the Spirit of adoption" when he wrote, For as many as are led by the Spirit of God, these are sons of God. For you did not receive the spirit of bondage again to fear, but you received the Spirit of adoption by whom we cry out, "Abba, Father." The Spirit Himself bears witness with our spirit that we are children of God (Romans 8:14–16).

Jesus said, God is Spirit, and those who worship Him must worship in spirit and truth (John 4:24).

God Is in Us

At the moment of salvation, Jesus comes into us! Behold, I stand at the door and knock. If anyone hears My voice and opens the door, I will come in to him and dine with him, and he with Me (Revelation 3:20).

The Holy Spirit is in us! Do you not know that you are the temple of God and that the Spirit of God dwells in you? (1 Corinthians 3:16).

Or do you not know that your body is the temple of the Holy Spirit who is in you, whom you have from God, and you are not your own? (1 Corinthians 6:19).

God is in us! One God and Father of all, who is above all, and through all, and in you all (Ephesians 4:6).

We keep hearing people say, "I'm just a normal believer." There is no such being. If we are believers, God is in us, and that's not normal! At the moment of salvation we move out of the arena of "normal," and we become the children of God. We move out of the realm of the natural and into the realm of the supernatural.

The greatest miracle of all is God, through His Son Jesus, bringing the gift of salvation. God taking the prostitutes, the pimps, the murderers, the alcoholics, the despondent, the drug addicts, the hard-driving businesspeople, the young, the old, people from all nationalities, and turning them into living spirits, His children — that's the greatest miracle of all.

Hearing and Communing with God

The first thing new members in the family of God need to know is how to hear from God. He is Spirit, and we must come to Him in the Spirit. Many times, when we have prayed, we have been talking *at* God. We haven't been conversing *with* Him.

When I was little, my mother used to sing the words to the hymn, *I Come to the Garden Alone*: "I come to the garden alone, While the dew is still on the roses....And He walks with me, and He talks with me, And He tells me I am His own."

This song painted such a wonderful picture in my imagination. I remember one day asking my mother why we couldn't do that. "Why doesn't Jesus walk in the garden with us?"

She replied, "Jesus is in heaven, and we're on earth. He can't come and walk with us anymore. He only talks to us through the Bible." Seeing my stricken expression, she continued, with longing in her voice, "It would be wonderful if He could."

How sad! As a little girl, I was reaching out to know God in a personal way, but I was told it wasn't possible. And even though I had asked Jesus to come into my heart, I didn't know we could have a personal relationship with Him.

Without my realizing it, that conversation became one of the guiding points in my life. To satisfy my inner desire to know Him, I became a student of His Word, but I never expected it to come alive to me. I prayed, but I never expected Him to answer, certainly not with words that I could hear. I talked to Him, but I never listened for His reply. I loved Him, but I never expected to feel His love in return. What an empty, one-sided relationship I had with God.

But that day, when God supernaturally stopped our car, He became alive to us. He wasn't just in heaven. He was all around us. He was in us!

When we were baptized in the Holy Spirit and lost our jobs, our church, and most of our friends all at one time, it was hard. I went through a period of grief. When things seemed about to overwhelm me in the natural, I would wonder what my spirit was doing and would be able to listen inside myself, and I would hear my spirit singing praises to the Lord.

I had known intellectually that I was spirit, soul, and body, but for the first time, the reality that I have a spirit was more than just words to me.

In the natural, we're in touch with our bodies. They tell us when they're cold, hungry, or hurting with no problem. But some of us have never come in contact with our spirits. You may be saying, "Well, this sounds good, but how do I do that?"

"You Don't Listen!"

When we received the baptism in the Holy Spirit, A.L. immediately began to hear God speaking. God even gave him the outline for whole sermons, reference by reference.

I wasn't hearing from God, and I became very frustrated about it. "God, why don't I hear from you?" I prayed many times. Finally, one day when I was praying another variation of this prayer, I heard from God. It was so exciting to me!

What did I hear God say the very first time I knew His voice? He said, "You don't listen!"

My Sheep Know My Voice

Jesus said, "My sheep know My voice."

It's a fact. His sheep know His voice.

Once, when we were in the Colorado Mountains, we looked way across the valley and saw a shepherd leading his sheep along the trail. He was walking ahead of them, crooning to them. His voice was soft, but when we listened, we heard it all the way across the valley. Of course, his sheep knew his voice. They heard it every day, all day.

In Jesus' time, the sheep from a whole village were brought together into a safe place with walls for the night. In the morning, the sheep were mixed together. But each shepherd would call to his own sheep, and they would follow their shepherd's voice out of the sheepfold.

Sheep know the voice of their shepherd, because they spend time with him, and because he talks to them.

Take Time

Soon after we received the baptism in the Holy Spirit, a friend gave us a message from God in a song with the words, "Take time to listen…Take time to pray…Take time to hear from Me…Open your spiritual ears."

We hear God's voice when we come into a personal relationship with Him, when we spend time talking with Him (not praying at Him in a one-sided conversation), when we study His written Word expecting Him to make it come alive, and by meditating on His Word.

Many times we want to hear from God when everything is a mess and we are desperate for direction. At those times we may be too anxious to hear clearly. It's far better to learn to hear from Him in the quiet times, so that we will know His voice in times of stress.

One of the best ways to become quiet before God is to pray and praise Him in the Spirit. When we do that, we stop trying to tell Him our desires and our plans, and we hear from Him.

Many times God awakens us in the middle of the night to talk to us. During the day, our minds have been busy and full of natural thoughts, and we haven't taken time to get quiet and listen to Him. At other times, we hear God's thoughts of guidance for the day when we first wake up in the morning. And often throughout the day, God interrupts our natural flow of thoughts and speaks to us.

The Miracle of Relationship with God

Again, the greatest miracle of all is God bringing us into His kingdom. It is God changing us from the natural to the supernatural. It is God bringing us into a new relationship with Himself, a relationship in which we have rights and privileges, a relationship in which we can talk to the Creator of the whole universe and He answers, a relationship of deep and intimate communion with God.

The Church Begins
in Power

The Church Begins in Power

A Village Turns to Jesus

The sun was setting over a beautiful beach area in southern India. The people had never seen electric lights such as the portable generator was making possible, and thousands gathered to see this wonder and to hear the music that was also coming from our system. These people had never heard the name of Jesus. They had never seen a Bible. Soon A.L. was preaching, and he couldn't say, "The Bible says… " because they didn't know what a Bible was. Why would they believe him?

He taught the Gospel in the simplest terms he knew. And then, at the prompting of God, he said, "God wants to confirm my words. He wants you to know that Jesus is His Son. And so that you will know He is the one and only, true and living God, He is going to heal all of you!"

A.L. was shocked at his own words! He had been meditating earlier that day on the times in the Bible when Jesus healed them all, and it was as if these words unintentionally slipped from the verses he had been meditating on into his preaching.

God is so faithful. As hundreds came forward, A.L. and others with him ministered to them, and everyone was healed! Backs were healed. Lungs were healed. Eyes were healed. As they ministered healing that night, they all knew there was no miracle too big for God.

After the people were healed, A.L. asked them to sit back down. He talked to them again about Jesus being the Son of God who was sent to earth to bring them salvation. He told them they must renounce all other gods. Thinking there might be a small number of them who would do that, he asked, "Is there anyone here who would like to accept Jesus as Savior?"

They all stood up!

A.L. thought, I must not have made it clear enough. He asked them all to sit back down. Again he explained it, being even more careful to make it clear. Again he asked if anyone would like to renounce their gods and accept Jesus as their only God and Savior.

They all stood up!

Thinking they had still misunderstood him, A.L. had them all sit down. He went through God's plan of salvation and the necessity of renouncing all other idols for the third time! He was even more clear in explaining every area of salvation.

Again, they all stood up to accept Jesus as Savior! A whole village passed from death to life because God had confirmed His Word with signs and wonders.

The Indian pastors who were with A.L. on that visit immediately made plans to start a church in that village.

*T*he Church Age began in the midst of many miraculous signs and wonders. In Acts, chapter three, we read of the lame man who was healed in the name of Jesus, and how, as a result of that miracle, five thousand believed and were saved!

Following this, what did the religious leaders demand? "Stop using the name of Jesus!" What did these believers do?

They prayed for even more boldness to keep on speaking in the name of Jesus with manifestations of healings, signs, and wonders.

Paul declared that his teaching and preaching were accompanied by demonstrations of the Spirit and the power of God. This was evidenced throughout his ministry when God worked extraordinary miracles through his hands. It was repeatedly evidenced when people were healed and delivered from demons – even when handkerchiefs and aprons were taken from Paul's body and laid on the sick and demon-possessed.

What an example the apostle Paul is to us! As he taught the Word to the believers in Ephesus and signs and wonders confirmed the Word he preached, everyone in Asia Minor heard the Word of the Lord.

Jesus didn't say these signs would follow only the apostles, evangelists, or other preachers. He said these signs would follow those who believe.

Signs accompanied Philip, who was a deacon in the Jerusalem church, when he preached in Samaria. Demons came out screaming, and the paralyzed and the lame were healed, resulting in great joy in that city. God was working with him, confirming His Word with signs.

God's plan for His people hasn't changed. We are all commissioned to believe His Word and share the Gospel with the lost. We are to expect Him to work with us, confirming His Word with signs wherever we go.

I Will Build My Church

Jesus said He would build a church, not churches. He didn't say He was going to build an early church full of faith, power, miracles, signs, and wonders, and then later build another church full of programs, entertainment, and committees. The church that we see in the book of Acts is the same church He is building today.

For too long, mankind has been trying to build the church with methods and programs, and this church has failed to reach the world with the true Gospel of Jesus.

The book of Acts is not to be studied as just the history of the early church. It was written as a supernatural pattern for our lives, ministries, and churches today. If the traditional patterns for our churches don't agree with these patterns, we need to lay aside our traditions and say, "Please, Jesus, build Your church in our midst!"

The story of the church starts with the book of Acts, and it starts with power. In Acts, chapter one, the believers were given two promises. One was the coming of the Holy Spirit, and the other was the return of our Lord and Savior. When the disciples saw Jesus go up into the clouds, the angels came and gave them the message of His coming again.

None of these things are of the natural human nature. They cannot be understood in the natural. They must be accepted by faith.

Jesus came as a baby born in a manger, but the Holy Spirit came in power. He came with the sound of a mighty rushing wind, with divided tongues of fire – giving power, boldness to be witnesses, and new languages to 120 believers.

Immediately after being baptized with the Holy Spirit, Peter, who had just weeks before denied Christ three times, was out on the street preaching to the multitudes, and three thousand people were saved.

Then in Acts, chapter three, we are told about the miracle of the lame man being healed. "In the name of Jesus, rise up and walk!" Peter said. And the man went walking, leaping, and praising God. What was the result? Five thousand souls were added to the church.

The Power of the Spirit
Flowing Through Believers

The phrase "Miracle Evangelism" is strong, and it is an apt description of the early church. The New Testament is the story of the power of the Holy Spirit flowing through believers.

Peter walked in power. God opened the prison doors for him. Multitudes were healed by his passing shadow. Ananias and Sapphira dropped dead at his word. What was the result?

Great fear came upon all the church and upon all who heard these things. And through the hands of the apostles many signs and wonders were done among the people....And believers were increasingly added to the Lord, multitudes of both men and women (Acts 5:11–12, 14).

Through Peter's prayers, Dorcas was raised from the dead, and it became known throughout all Joppa, and many believed on the Lord (Acts 9:42).

Peter received a vision from God on a rooftop in Joppa that set him free from legalistic traditions that would have hindered him from reaching the Gentiles with the Gospel.

God has a supernatural plan, a power plan, for the growth of His church. It is the same plan that we see happening in the book of Acts. It is easily found. Jesus said, I will build My church (Matthew 16:18).

The church was not to build itself. Jesus was, and is, to build it, and it will be a church of power. It will be a church of believers, operating as commissioned by Jesus and empowered by the Holy Spirit.

Jesus' plan includes every believer. His followers are to be witnesses. You shall receive power when the Holy Spirit has come upon you; and you shall be witnesses to Me in Jerusalem, and in all Judea and Samaria, and to the end of the earth (Acts 1:8).

They are to do the things Jesus did. They are to preach, to proclaim, to share the Gospel.

According to Ephesians, chapter four, believers, not just ministry leaders, are to be discipled and equipped to do the works of the ministry. The leaders are to train and equip all believers, and all leaders and believers are to do the works of Jesus. Leaders cannot fulfill the Great Commission by themselves, and believers cannot fulfill it without being equipped.

Let's go back to the life of Paul. It was certainly filled with the power of the Holy Spirit. We have the accounts of his marvelous conversion on the road to Damascus and his being filled with the Holy Spirit through the hands of Ananias. We read how he was blind for three days, but was healed through the laying on of hands.

When Elymas the sorcerer tried to prevent the proconsul from hearing the Gospel, Paul, filled with the Holy Spirit, looked intently at him and said, "O full of all deceit and all fraud, you son of the devil, you enemy of all righteousness, will you not cease perverting the straight ways of the Lord? And now, indeed, the hand of the Lord is upon you, and you shall be blind, not seeing the sun for a time." And immediately a dark mist fell on him, and he went around seeking someone to lead him by the hand. Then the proconsul believed, when he saw what had been done, being astonished (Acts 13:9–12).

Paul spoke to the lame man in Lystra, "Stand up straight on your feet!" And he leaped and walked (Acts 14:10).

Paul brought deliverance to the slave girl possessed with the spirit of divination.

Locked in a Philippian dungeon, he was set free by a supernatural earthquake.

While Paul was preaching, Eutychus went to sleep, fell from a third-story window, and died! But Paul rushed down the stairs, fell on him, embraced him, and brought him back to life.

On the island of Malta, a venomous snake bit Paul, but he shook if off into the fire and was unharmed.

That was the beginning of the church, but what about the church today?

Churches to Be Built

In a desire to be "seeker friendly," many churches have laid aside the gifts of the Holy Spirit, the signs, wonders, and miracles, so as not to offend. Many have even forbidden speaking in tongues in the church. But Jesus said speaking in tongues is a sign that will follow those who believe. And Paul wrote, Therefore tongues are for a sign, not to those who believe but to unbelievers. To be even clearer, he continued, Do not forbid to speak with tongues (1 Corinthians 14:22, 39).

The things of the Spirit are foolish to the natural mind. The natural man does not receive the things of the Spirit of God, for they are foolishness to him; nor can he know them, because they are spiritually discerned (1 Corinthians 2:14).

The natural mind thinks we should forbid speaking in tongues because unbelievers would be offended. And yet, on the Day of Pentecost, when 120 believers were all speaking in other tongues, three thousand people were saved.

The natural mind thinks people would be offended if our lives, ministries, and churches were full of signs, wonders, and healing miracles. But Jesus said that laying our hands on the sick and seeing them recover would be a sign that would follow those who believe. These healings would be important signs to confirm His Word.

In past moves of the Spirit, singular mighty men and women of God have been used to exhibit signs, wonders, and healing miracles. However, a major shift is taking place in evangelism. Believers are beginning to understanding that every believer can do the same works that Jesus did! God is extending miracle evangelism from the hands of anointed healing ministers into the hands of "ordinary" Spirit-filled believers.

It's easy to let the supernatural gifts of the Spirit drift away when we become busy with our church programs and the daily affairs of life. But God's Word admonishes us, Therefore we must give the more earnest heed to the things we have heard, lest we drift away (Hebrews 2:1).

Paul wrote to Timothy, Therefore I remind you to stir up the gift of God which is in you through the laying on of my hands (2 Timothy 1:6).

When Jesus commissioned us to go into all the world and preach the gospel to every creature, He said, These signs will follow those who believe (Mark 16:15, 17).

What are the signs He mentioned? They include casting out demons, speaking in new tongues, and laying hands on the sick with the sick recovering. Jesus also said these signs were given to confirm God's Word when we preach the Gospel in the power of His Holy Spirit.

The church that Jesus is building isn't to be built on our traditions or what seems reasonable to our natural minds. It's to be built on demonstrations of the Spirit and of the power of God.

We've Been Conned!

CHAPTER SEVEN

We've Been Conned!

Turning the Storm

We had joined some very good friends for a series of meetings in San Diego, California, and we had seen wonderful healing miracles in the meeting that night. We were excitedly sharing one miracle after another in their hotel room.

But somehow, my attention was drawn to the news being given on television. There had been weeks of rain in San Diego, and that day they were showing pictures of houses, caught in awful mudslides, sliding down the hillsides. The news commentator continued telling about another storm that was going to hit the city that night.

"You know," I said, "we can stop that storm." But no one heard me. They hadn't joined me when I had turned my attention to the news.

"We can stop that storm!" I tried again. But I still didn't make myself heard.

"That storm must not hit San Diego," I stated emphatically. But still they continued talking excitedly about the miracles that had happened.

By now, I felt such urgency in my spirit that I couldn't wait to get anyone to join me. Turning in my chair and pointing in the direction of the ocean and the storm, I started, "In the name of Jesus..."

Silence filled the room for a second, and then all three of them joined me. "In the name of Jesus, storm, I take authority over you! You cannot hit San Diego!"

The headlines the next morning read, "Storm Veers Suddenly to the North and Misses San Diego."

Why was I so concerned, when the others were not? Why did I feel an urgency to take authority over that storm? The answer is simple. I had heard from God.

Oh, the marvelous things that God can do as believers start actually hearing and doing the works of Jesus!

*W*hen we read of the exploits of the early believers, we should have a burning desire to know God in the same way they did. Where is the courage of Stephen to face martyrdom? Where is the strength of the apostle Paul to face the continuous hardships of ministry? Where are the miracles we read about in the book of Acts when believers took the message of Jesus to the world?

Satan has infiltrated the church. His deceptions have been taught for so long that believers actually feel more comfortable accepting these things as truth than they do in believing the Word of God.

In the past, A.L. and I were taught that the Bible doesn't mean what it seems to say in many places and that we must understand the original language to know what God meant. And yet, we declared, "We believe the Word of God."

How often we have heard Christians (notice we're not using the word *believers* here) make statements like, "Oh, I couldn't heal a flea." "I wouldn't presume to say I could heal the sick." "I'm not that proud. Jesus wants us to be humble."

But Jesus commanded, "Heal the sick!" These same words are recorded one time in Matthew and two times in Luke (Matthew 10:8; Luke 9:2; 10:9).

When we insist we cannot do what Jesus said we are to do, we are in rebellion against the Word of God. Of course, most of us are not doing this in deliberate rebellion. We've been convinced, in mistaken humility, that we are just poor lost sinners saved by grace. The truth is that we *were* poor lost sinners, past tense. But once we have accepted Jesus as our Lord and Savior, we *are* new creations. We have come into a personal relationship with God.

The church of our tradition was so busy telling us what we couldn't do that we never heard what we could do. Being evangelistic in nature, our pastors continuously preached to the sinners. We read our Bibles, we went to Bible school, but somehow the words we read, which didn't agree with our doctrines, were never noticed. Our doctrines blinded us to the truth.

Statements saying we can never do the works of Jesus are expressions of false humility. They are a lie of Satan. The Bible says we can.

Another belief Satan has propagated throughout the church is the division between the ministry and "ordinary believers." We have been led to believe that only certain ministries can do certain things.

First, Jesus sent the twelve out to heal the sick, cleanse the lepers, raise the dead, cast out demons (Matthew 10:8). "Oh," we can say, "we're not one of the original twelve disciples. This verse couldn't apply to us."

But Jesus also sent out seventy believers to heal the sick there, and say to them, "The kingdom of God has come near to you" (Luke 10:9). "Well," we might reply, "that's not in our time. That was in a different dispensation."

And then, just before Jesus left this earth, when His church was about to be established, He said to them, "Go into all the world and preach the gospel to every creature....And these signs will follow those who believe: In My name they will cast out demons; they will speak with new tongues; they will take up serpents; and if they drink anything deadly, it will by no means hurt them; they will lay hands on the sick, and they will recover" (Mark 16:15, 17–18).

To whom was Jesus speaking? Those who believe. If we are believers, Jesus was speaking to us!

Satan has effectively tied believers into knots by reminding them of all the horrible things they have done in the past. He has put guilt, shame, and condemnation on them. He has gotten them so preoccupied with all the problems in their own lives that they have had no time to reach out to the world with the wonderful message of salvation provided through Jesus.

In looking at their own problems, they have lost the joy of their salvation. And in losing their joy, they have lost the very thing the world is meant to see and hunger for.

We used to quote the saying, "God's in His heaven, and all's right with the world." But all isn't right with our world. Distress, sickness, and disease are all around us. We are the body of Christ on earth, and we are to minister to those we come in contact with.

God Wants His People to Move in the Supernatural

God desires that every believer move in the supernatural. There were many incidents of God being involved in our lives before He supernaturally stopped our car in 1968, but we never recognized them as such. Our erroneous doctrines had become blindfolds hiding the truth from us.

About 11:30 one night, when we were getting into bed, I suddenly knew a terrible thing was about to happen to A.L.'s dad. "A.L.," I shouted, "something's going to happen to your dad. Call him right now! The ringing will stop it!"

A.L. leaped out of bed and ran for the telephone, and I stayed in bed asking God what was wrong. How could the ringing of the telephone help?

Now, as I look back, I know I was seeing in the Spirit when I saw what looked like a black tornado by a certain window in A.L.'s parents' home. I saw the silhouette of Dad coming out of their bedroom with a gun in his hand. Then I heard the telephone ring and watched the evil tornado (the intruder) flee in the opposite direction.

Perhaps the would-be intruder thought a neighbor had seen him and called to warn the family. Perhaps he knew the family would now be awake. Whatever the reason, I knew the ringing of the phone had prevented a tragedy from happening.

After A.L. called, Dad checked each window in the house to be sure it was locked. He found one unlocked window, and that was exactly where I had seen the danger.

Satan's plan was to kill Dad that night, but God intervened!

Faith Is More than Facts

The transition from mental belief in God's Word to moving in His Spirit was not an easy one for us. We had been trained all our lives that it was what you knew that was important.

We had been taught facts, but we had never been taught faith. We would read verses, but if they didn't line up with our theology, we didn't see them. And we didn't even realize we were doing this. All during this time, we stated often,

"We believe every word of the Bible." We called ourselves believers, but we spent most of our time being doubters.

We called ourselves children of God, but we missed the importance of a relationship with Him. For the most part, we studied the new birth as an escape from the judgment of hell and so that we could go to heaven when we died.

We didn't understand that, at the moment of salvation, we were literally born again. We passed from being in only the natural realm, to also being in the supernatural realm. We passed into the realm of the Spirit.

We Can Change the World Because of Who We Are in Christ

Too many of us still picture ourselves in the book of Isaiah. We are all like an unclean thing, and all our righteousnesses are like filthy rags; we all fade as a leaf, and our iniquities, like the wind, have taken us away (Isaiah 64:6).

Yet, the apostle Paul wrote, Therefore, if anyone is in Christ, he is a new creation; old things have passed away; behold, all things have become new (2 Corinthians 5:17).

The old filthy rags are gone. We have gotten rid of our iniquities, and all things have become new.

Paul continued, For He made Him who knew no sin to be sin for us, that we might become the righteousness of God in Him (2 Corinthians 5:21).

What a marvelous exchange! Jesus took our sins so that He might give us His righteousness! He took our inabilities and gave us His abilities. He took our judgment and gave us His authority. He took our weak human bodies and made us part of His body.

When Satan says to us, "You can't do that!" we reply, "Yes, we can! We can do all things through Jesus Christ who strengthens us" (Philippians 4:13).

86

We can see miracles happen because Jesus said we could. It's not in our strength, but in His. It's not in our righteousness, but in His. We can change our world, not because of who we are in ourselves, but because of who we are in Him!

CHAPTER EIGHT

Moving in the Supernatural

Chapter Eight

Moving in the Supernatural

Supernatural Travel

Soon after we received the baptism in the Holy Spirit, we went to our church one Sunday morning, and then we were planning to join my sister and her family for dinner afterward. During Sunday school, I felt normal, but when I walked into the auditorium for the church service, an unbelievable pain hit my head. I stopped walking, and A.L. turned to me and asked what was wrong. I barely whispered, "Please take me home."

When we got there, I crawled into bed and went to sleep almost instantly. Our children were in Children's Church, so A.L. went back for the service and to pick them up.

At ten minutes to twelve, the Lord woke me up. "Get up and dressed," He said.

When A.L. came home with the family, he was surprised to see me dressed and ready to go. "We can call them and cancel," he said. But God had told me to get ready.

I felt fine while we drove to their home, but when I walked in their front door, the same pain hit me again. This time, it hit so hard I staggered into their living room. What could be wrong? This wasn't a normal headache.

This was the same living room where A.L. had been healed several years before, and the four of us immediately started praying for my healing. As we prayed, a strong heat burned through my body, and it continued to burn for several hours. It was uncomfortable, but not painful, and I was completely healed of whatever had caused the terrible headache.

The children kept touching me to feel the heat. It was radiating off my body and could be felt about a foot away. The rest of the family had dinner, but I was in a world of my own. I knew what was going on, but I didn't seem to care.

Later, we were talking in the living room, the heat was still in me, and God said, "Go home." Immediately, we called our children and left. The day had been so unusual. God didn't usually tell us when to leave, and A.L. made a special note of the time as we climbed into the car.

I was still in my own world while A.L. drove home, and didn't notice anything unusual. Neither did A.L., until he was pulling into our driveway. As he stopped the car, he thought, I can't remember much of the drive home. I remember pulling onto the freeway, but nothing after that until I pulled into our driveway. He looked at his watch, and it was just twelve minutes later than when we had left my sister's home. A trip that usually takes about an hour had taken twelve minutes!

We had been supernaturally translated, much like Philip in the book of Acts. We read in Acts, **Now when they came up out of the water, the Spirit of the Lord caught Philip away, so that the eunuch saw him no more; and he went on his way rejoicing. But Philip was found at Azotus (Acts 8:39–40).**

*E*lisha walked with Elijah. He knew Elijah. He saw him perform miracles. And his prayer became, "Let me have double the anointing. Let me do twice as many miracles."

What did Elijah tell him? "If you see me leave, you will have the double anointing." That seems hard. "If you see me go, you will have your prayer answered."

Why did Elijah tell him that? Was it just to make it hard for Elisha? No. Why, then? I pondered this question for many years, but when the answer came, it was very simple.

Miracles happen in the supernatural realm, in the realm of the Spirit. If Elisha was going to receive the double anointing, he had to see into the Spirit-realm. He had to hear from God and know what was going to happen in the future. Two times, Elisha told the sons of the prophets that he knew Elijah was going to be with the Lord that day.

What did he cry out when the chariot of fire appeared and Elijah left? "My father, my father, the chariot of Israel and its horsemen!" (2 Kings 2:12). He saw them. He saw into the Spirit-realm. He had moved from the natural to the supernatural, and he received the double anointing he had asked for.

Later, Elisha prayed that the eyes of his servant might be opened. And when the servant of the man of God arose early and went out, there was an army, surrounding the city with horses and chariots. And his servant said to him, "Alas, my master! What shall we do?"

So he answered, "Do not fear, for those who are with us are more than those who are with them."

And Elisha prayed, and said, "LORD, I pray, open his eyes that he may see." Then the LORD opened the eyes of the young man, and he saw. And behold, the mountain was full of horses and chariots of fire all around Elisha (2 Kings 6:15–17).

"Lord, Open Our Eyes"

Our prayer has become, "Lord, open our eyes so that we may see. Let us view our lives from your viewpoint. Let us view our problems in the light of all eternity."

There is the natural realm, where we live, move, breathe, study, work, and have our families and friends. This is all temporal. It's limited by time. And there is the super-natural realm, the Spirit-realm, where eternity is.

We live in the temporal for a certain number of years, and then we "die" and move into the Spirit-realm for all eternity. Because we see and experience the natural, we tend to think it's the most important. Perhaps it is, because we certainly make decisions in the temporal realm that will affect us for all eternity.

But entering the new birth means that we move from being only in the natural realm to also being in the Spirit-realm. From the moment of salvation on, we have "dual citizenship." We are part of the natural, but we are also part of the supernatural.

The new birth means coming into a new family, the family of God. It means coming into a relationship with God.

The Role of Faith

The new birth means coming to the place where we can say, "Abba, Father."

This relationship cannot be understood with the natural mind; it must be accepted by faith. It is hearing and reading the Word, realizing God's Word is true, and giving mental assent to it. But it is more than this. It can only be experienced when we move into the Spirit-realm of God.

It can only be experienced when we stop trying to understand and just believe — when we simply have faith. The writer of Hebrews wrote, **Now faith is the substance of things hoped for, the evidence of things not seen (Hebrews 11:1).**

The word *substance* has meanings that we may be missing. This verse could be restated in these ways: Faith is the firm foundation; faith is that which has actual existence;

faith is real; faith is a steadfastness of mind; faith is firmness, courage, and resolution.

Faith is given to every human being. Paul wrote, God has dealt to each one a measure of faith (Romans 12:3).

Paul also wrote that our faith can be increased: …as your faith is increased, we shall be greatly enlarged by you in our sphere (2 Corinthians 10:15).

The writer of the book of Hebrews said, Without faith it is impossible to please Him, for he who comes to God must believe that He is, and that He is a rewarder of those who diligently seek Him (Hebrews 11:6).

"But," you may be asking, "how do we get faith?" The apostle Paul answered that question, too: So then faith comes by hearing, and hearing by the word of God (Romans 10:17).

In the Greek language, the word that we hear that brings faith is *rhema*. Faith comes by hearing, and hearing the *rhema* of God. As we read, study, and meditate on the *logos*, that is, the written Word of God, suddenly God speaks a personal *rhema* into our spirits. In that instant, faith leaps into our spirits.

Too many times we have read the Bible to prove what we believe. We have read it from the viewpoint of our own convictions. Instead, we are to read it and say, "Yes, Lord. Amen. I agree!"

The apostle Paul wrote of this when he said, For all the promises of God in Him are Yes, and in Him Amen, to the glory of God through us (2 Corinthians 1:20).

The word *faith* is used 227 times in the New Testament. Living a life of faith – living a life of believing in God and in His Word – is the entranceway to moving into the supernatural.

Doubt and unbelief are the enemies of faith. Jesus had perfect, undiluted faith, and yet even His works were limited by the doubt and unbelief of others.

Jesus said to them, "A prophet is not without honor [or esteem] except in his own country, among his own relatives, and in his own house."

Now He could do no mighty work there, except that He laid His hands on a few sick people and healed them. And He marveled because of their unbelief (Mark 6:4–6).

Because they knew Jesus in the natural – He was one of them – they didn't accept Him in the supernatural. Their unbelief kept Him from doing miracles in their midst.

Jesus marveled at the centurion's faith. He told the woman with the issue of blood that her faith had made her well. He told the blind men that it would be to them according to their faith, and they were healed. He spoke to the Canaanite woman, "O woman, great is your faith! Let it be to you as you desire" (Matthew 15:28).

Several times, Jesus chided the disciples for their lack of faith. He said, "O you of little faith." He even asked them, "Where is your faith?" And one time, Jesus pointed out to them that they were reasoning instead of believing: He said to them, "O you of little faith, why do you reason among yourselves...?" (Matthew 16:8).

Move into the Supernatural Realm Through Faith

Doubt is sin. It is contrary to the Word of God. Worry is sin. It is contrary to the Word of God. Unbelief is sin. It is contrary to the Word of God. It's time we recognize these "human frailties" for what they are – sin – and confess our sins before God so that we can go on to live a life of faith.

We can only move into the supernatural realm of God when we move in faith.

CHAPTER NINE

The Choice Is Ours

The Choice Is Ours

Miracle in the Basement

A.L. was out of the country, and I was on an aluminum ladder putting plastic over a window down in the basement.

I was using a staple gun that you swing much like a hammer and making good time on the project, when I looked back and realized I had missed an area of stapling. Rather than climbing down and moving the ladder over, I stretched back and swung the stapler. The force of it hitting the beam caused me to lose my balance, and I started to fall.

The human mind is such a marvelous instrument. In times of danger, it can work at unbelievable speed. Of course, I grabbed for the ladder, but it was of such a light weight that it started falling with me. I looked at the concrete steps where I would land. I was alone — there was no telephone in the basement — and it might be days before anyone would miss me. These thoughts were racing through my mind while I was still falling.

I remember making a decision. In the natural, it made no sense at all. But I decided, I'm not going to fall!

The next thing I knew, I was back standing on the ladder. It was standing upright once more, and I was shaking violently from head to toe.

I hadn't fallen!

I can't tell you what happened when I said, "I'm not going to fall!" But I do know that God had once again intervened!

*W*hen God created Adam and Eve, He created them with the ability to make choices. He did not create them to be robots, to operate automatically without original thoughts. He did not create them to be "puppets on a string," completely controlled by a Higher Being.

When God put the Tree of Knowledge of Good and Evil in the Garden and told Adam he could not eat from it, He gave mankind the ability to choose. They could obey God's instructions or disobey. God gave them each a free will.

As we know, they chose to disobey God, and the world has been in trouble ever since. From that time until now, everything in life has been a choice.

God created the world, and then God created man in His own image; in the image of God He created him; male and female He created them. Then God blessed them, and God said to them, "Be fruitful and multiply; fill the earth and subdue it; have dominion over the fish of the sea, over the birds of the air, and over every living thing that moves on the earth" (Genesis 1:27–28).

God has given us the ability to choose, and He has given us the right to rule on this earth.

"Choose for Yourselves This Day"

Joshua made a great choice when he said, And if it seems evil to you to serve the LORD, choose for yourselves this day whom you will serve,...but as for me and my house, we will serve the LORD (Joshua 24:15).

It was written of Moses, **By faith Moses, when he became** of age, refused to be called the son of Pharaoh's daughter, choosing rather to suffer affliction with the people of God than to enjoy the passing pleasures of sin (Hebrews 11:24–25).

David wrote, I have chosen the way of truth; Your judgments I have laid before me (Psalm 119:30).

"Well," you might say, "what about people all around the world who are being imprisoned because they are Christians?" That is still a result of their choices, good choices. They have chosen to serve God no matter what the cost.

Job didn't understand what was happening in his life. He blamed God for what Satan was doing, and yet he still said, Though He slay me, yet will I trust Him (Job 13:15). Job had made a choice to trust God.

In talking to Mary and Martha, Jesus said, "Martha, Martha, you are worried and troubled about many things. But one thing is needed, and Mary has chosen that good part, which will not be taken away from her" (Luke 10:41–42).

Consequences of Our Choices

Not all choices are good. What about Jonah saying, "I'm not going to go to Nineveh," and getting on a ship heading in the opposite direction? The storm came up; he was thrown overboard and went to live in the belly of a huge fish. We could all say, "Bad choice, Jonah." But what happened when he repented? God had that fish vomit him right out on the shores of Nineveh!

We tend to think of the apostle Paul as a saint, as one who could make no errors in judgment. But let's look at the choice he made in chapters twenty-one and twenty-two of Acts. First, we read that in Tyre, they [the disciples] told Paul through the Spirit not to go up to Jerusalem (Acts 21:4). The Holy Spirit warned Paul, "Don't go to Jerusalem."

Then, later, while Paul was in Caesarea, we read, As we stayed many days, a certain prophet named Agabus came down from Judea. When he had come to us, he took Paul's belt, bound his own hands and feet, and said, "Thus says the Holy Spirit, 'So shall the Jews at Jerusalem bind the man who owns this belt, and deliver him into the hands of the Gentiles'" (Acts 21:10–11).

God sent a second warning to Paul and told him what would happen if he did go to Jerusalem. He even sent one recognized as a prophet to come from another city.

But Paul answered, I am ready not only to be bound, but also to die at Jerusalem for the name of the Lord Jesus (Acts 21:13).

Agabus didn't say Paul was going to die. He said he would be bound.

So when he would not be persuaded, we ceased, saying, "The will of the Lord be done" (Acts 21:14).

Paul went on to Jerusalem, and he did present Jesus to the crowds, but let's listen to his own words: Now it happened, when I returned to Jerusalem and was praying in the temple, that I was in a trance and saw Him saying to me, "Make haste and get out of Jerusalem quickly, for they will not receive your testimony concerning Me" (Acts 22:17–18).

God warned Paul the third time! Get out of Jerusalem quickly! But what did Paul do?

So I said, "Lord, they know that in every synagogue I imprisoned and beat those who believe on You. And when the blood of Your martyr Stephen was shed, I also was standing by consenting to his death, and guarding the clothes of those who were killing him" (Acts 22:19–20).

God is so faithful! He spoke to Paul one more time. We read again in Paul's own words, Then He said to me, "Depart, for I will send you far from here to the Gentiles" (Acts 22:21).

God said, "Don't go to Jerusalem." And then He said, "Get out of Jerusalem," and He even continued to tell Paul His plan for his life.

But Paul still chose to go to Jerusalem in spite of the warnings he had received from others who had heard from God. He chose to stay in Jerusalem even when warned again in a dream. And that was the beginning of Paul's many years of imprisonment.

We can see the mindset of Paul in several of his statements. The first was when he went from Agabus' warning of being bound to saying, "I'm ready to die for the name of Jesus." Then when he argued with God in the dream, he said, "I imprisoned others. I was there when Stephen was killed."

It appears Paul felt that since he had killed other believers, he deserved death. He was ready for death, but God had another plan for his life. God didn't need the Roman soldiers to arrest Paul to bring him to the Gentiles. That happened as a result of Paul's choices. God had said to Paul, "I will send you far from here to the Gentiles."

It's exciting to learn that, even though it looks to us that Paul made the wrong decisions and therefore was imprisoned first in Jerusalem, then in Caesarea, and finally in Rome, God was with him and used him at every step of the way. God's purpose for his life was still carried out. He still went far from Jerusalem to the Gentiles.

A Personal Choice

I made a bad choice years ago, and I didn't learn about it for several months, until God brought it back to my attention. I had been diagnosed as having cancer, and my first words were, "God, where did I open the door?" I didn't ask myself. I didn't ask A.L. I asked God, and He answered.

Instantly, it was as if I were back several months earlier, standing in my own living room. I had just purchased some luggage I had wanted, and it was spread out around me. I was figuring out how to use it, when I said to myself, I don't know why I bought that luggage. I don't want to travel. And I had then gathered it together and put it in the storage room.

Now I had cancer, and God took me back to that day. God, I thought, surely that decision wasn't serious enough to open the door to cancer!

Repentance Overcomes Rebellion

God had led us to travel, and I had made a statement that I didn't want to travel. That was rebellion. Because I had opened the door through disobedience, cancer came as the result. Of course, if I had cancer, no one would expect me to travel.

I decided at once that I would change my mind. I would travel. I repented of my attitude and of being in rebellion. Immediately, I asked for forgiveness, and God wonderfully, graciously forgave me and healed me of the cancer.

When we make decisions, we don't always understand the consequences.

Good Choices

But that's enough about bad choices. Let's think some more about the good choices. When we were driving up the mountain and A.L. was praying about the communion service where he was going to minister, God showed him the way He wanted us to take communion. When they brought out the small loaf of bread, A.L. had a choice. He could have thought, I guess I made a mistake. It couldn't have been God because He knew how small the loaf would be. He didn't do that! He went on with what God had said, and we all got to share in a special miracle.

Miracles are often missed because we haven't moved into the supernatural, because we haven't heard from God and obeyed Him.

God Doesn't Condemn Us for Our Bad Choices — He Forgives Us!

In teaching about choices, we know from experience what Satan's attack against you will be. At this point, he will probably be trying to put you under condemnation for the bad choices you have made in your life. The apostle John wrote, **God did not send His Son into the world to condemn the world, but that the world through Him might be saved** (John 3:17).

If the choices we have made in the past, like Paul's, have not always been the right choices, we may be bearing the consequences of them. But we can go on to live fulfilled lives, if we forgive others, forgive ourselves, and receive God's forgiveness.

God has given us such a wonderful promise, **We know that all things work together for good to those who love God, to those who are the called according to His purpose** (Romans 8:28).

God has given us free will. He has given us the right to choose, and He will never violate that right, even when He knows we are making a bad choice. If God did violate our wills, we wouldn't be free. We would be like puppets on a string.

When the children of Israel decided not to go into the Promised Land, God let them make that decision and wander in the wilderness for forty years. It certainly wasn't the best use of their lives. All but two of them died in the wilderness. But still, God let them do what they chose.

When we read God's Word, the choice is ours. We can see and believe the miracles, or we can pass over them. We can see the Bible as a wonderful Book of the supernatural, or we can continue to read it as history. We can come into a wonderful personal relationship with God, or we can worship Him from afar.

We can believe healing is for our time, or we can believe the gifts of healing have ceased. We can believe and receive healing, or we can doubt and do without healing. There is no condemnation either way.

God was speaking to the children of Israel when He said, I have set before you life and death, blessing and cursing; therefore choose life, that both you and your descendants may live (Deuteronomy 30:19).

Choose Life

Let's choose life. Let's choose blessings for both our children and ourselves. Let's say with Joshua, "As for me and my house, we will serve the Lord."

Let's choose faith. Every day is a new day with God. The past can be forgiven, and there is always a new path before us. We can believe and expect miracles to happen.

CHAPTER TEN

Ingredients to a Miracle

CHAPTER TEN

Ingredients to a Miracle

The Expectancy of Faith

Some good friends of ours were out of work, and they were driving a terrible car. If you stepped on the brakes too hard or hit a bump in the road, it would shudder and pull sideways. The only way you could stop the shaking was to come to a complete stop. It used almost as much oil as it did gasoline, and you could hear it coming from over a block away. It did get them around, and they were thankful for it, but it was a continuous reminder of how things were for them financially.

One evening, in our home prayer group, they asked A.L. to pray for the gas mileage of that car to be improved and for it not to use so much oil. We all bowed our heads expecting A.L. to pray. "No," he said, "I'm not going to do it!"

What? We always pray when people ask. We all opened our eyes and looked at him in shock. "Leon," he said, "God doesn't want you driving that old car. It isn't even safe! What kind of car would you like to have?"

"Any car," Leon answered. "Any car that would run better!"

"No!" A.L. replied, "Not any car! If you had your choice, what car would you like to have?"

Finally, Leon's wife, Betty, replied, "I've always wanted a Cadillac."

"No," Leon interjected. "What if God has a different car for us?"

"What color?" A.L. asked Betty.

"Any color God has!" Leon answered.

"Ah...I always wanted white," Betty put in softly.

"Okay," A.L. said, "now we can pray."

"Lord, we know that car they're driving isn't safe, and we ask that you give them a white Cadillac."

That was on a Tuesday night. On Sunday night, A.L. said, "Let's go see Betty and Leon's car." We drove to their home, and the car wasn't there.

"Leon," A.L. said, "where's your white Cadillac? Did you put it in the garage?"

"Uh...no. We haven't received it yet."

"That's no problem. You will," A.L. answered confidently.

Tuesday night, we were waiting for them to drive up in their new car, but soon we heard the rumble of the old one approaching. When they came in, A.L. asked, "Where's your new car?"

"I wish I knew!" Leon responded.

Then another member of the prayer group stood up, walked across the room, and handed the ownership papers of a beautiful white Cadillac to Leon and Betty. None of us knew they had a white Cadillac in their garage that they almost never drove. We had never seen it before.

God had used this time of specific prayer to show them He wanted them to give their car to Leon and Betty.

In discussing this later, I had to admit to A.L. that my faith had never been as strong as his for the new car. "Really?" he replied in surprise, "I heard from God. I knew they were going to get that car!"

Betty, Leon, and I were trying to believe. But because he had heard from God, A.L. believed.

*W*ow," you may be saying by this time. "I want miracles like this to happen in my life!" How do miracles happen? Sometimes we believe and pray for them, and sometimes they seem to happen spontaneously. But what allows a miracle to happen? What must we do to set the stage, or create the atmosphere, where miracles can happen?

Let's go back to the story of Jesus turning the water into wine at the wedding feast, the first miracle He did. Are there lessons in this event that will help us move into a miraculous way of living?

Identify the Problem

Now both Jesus and His disciples were invited to the wedding. And when they ran out of wine, the mother of Jesus said to Him, "They have no wine" (John 2:2–3).

Mary identified the problem.

One of the first ingredients to a miracle is to be clear about what we need. Many times when we pray, we aren't specific. Our prayers are so general that when they are answered, we don't recognize the answer.

Hearing and Obeying God

Then His mother said to the servants, "Whatever He says to you, do it" (John 2:5).

There are two ingredients to a miracle in this short sentence. The first is to hear from God – "Whatever He says." Notice that we aren't necessarily to understand it. The second is to obey – "Do it!"

Jesus said to them, "Fill the waterpots with water." And they filled them up to the brim. And He said to them, "Draw some out now, and take it to the master of the feast" (John 2:7–8).

When did the water actually turn to wine? The Bible doesn't say. In the natural, the servants had filled waterpots with water. Now came the real test of obedience: Take it to the master of the feast. If one person had hesitated and tested the miracle – "I think I'll take a little sip to be sure" – doubt and unbelief would have come in, and the miracle most likely wouldn't have happened. The servants had to be obedient and take it to the master of the feast. They had to act in faith.

And they took it. When the master of the feast had tasted the water that was made wine, and did not know where it came from (but the servants who had drawn the water knew), the master of the feast called the bridegroom. And he said to him, "Every man at the beginning sets out the good wine, and when the guests have well drunk, then the inferior. You have kept the good wine until now!" (John 2:8–10).

Jesus was, and is, our most wonderful example of a man, the Last Adam, working miracles. He gave us a strong indication of how we can work miracles, when He said, Most assuredly, I say to you, the Son can do nothing of Himself, but what He sees the Father do; for whatever He does, the Son also does in like manner (John 5:19).

We "see what the Father is doing" through the operation of the revelation gifts of the Holy Spirit. Sometimes, God will speak a few words into our spirits, and those few words will give us the next step. Sometimes, He gives us complete understanding of a situation. Sometimes we see, in the Spirit, ourselves or someone else doing something. The ways God speaks to us are endless.

Through the word of wisdom, we know or see that a miracle is going to take place before it happens. This releases the gift of faith. We boldly begin to do what we heard or saw God doing through us. And that is the working of miracles, another gift of the Holy Spirit.

Pray God's Will

Another ingredient to a miracle is to pray God's will. The apostle James wrote, You ask and do not receive, because you ask amiss (James 4:3).

When the disciples asked Jesus to teach them how to pray, He said, In this manner, therefore, pray: Our Father in heaven, hallowed be Your name. Your kingdom come. Your will be done on earth as it is in heaven (Matthew 6:9–10).

For miracles to happen, we cannot be concerned with what we want, with our own wills and desires. We must be concerned with His will.

So many times, when we pray, we are giving God a blueprint of how we think a situation should work out. Our prayers are: "God, please do this, and please do that."

But Jesus said we are to pray, "Our Father...Your will be done."

Steps to a Miracle

Over the years, A.L. and I have put together our own steps to a miracle, and we are including them here.

Understand There Are Causes and Effects

Most things don't just happen. If we don't understand the cause of our situation, we need to ask God for supernatural knowledge and understanding.

Facing ourselves honestly is important. We need to ask God, "Why am I in this situation? Have I been disobedient?

How did I miss You? What do I need to learn, repent of, or change in my life?"

David wrote, Search me, O God, and know my heart; try me, and know my anxieties; and see if there is any wicked way in me, and lead me in the way everlasting (Psalm 139:23–24).

Forgive Others and Ourselves

Forgiveness is an act of the will, not an emotion. We choose to forgive, regardless of how hurt we have been, how despicable the other person or persons are, or how tragic the situation is. We must forgive others and ourselves. We may even have to consciously release anger or bitterness that we have been harboring against God and ask His forgiveness for it, if we feel He let something happen that He could have prevented.

Jesus said, Whenever you stand praying, if you have anything against anyone, forgive him, that your Father in heaven may also forgive you your trespasses. But if you do not forgive, neither will your Father in heaven forgive your trespasses (Mark 11:25–26).

We cannot walk in the miraculous power of God and have unforgiveness in our lives. One is contrary to the other.

Meditate on God's Word Regarding Your Need

To meditate means to spend time thinking about, to ponder, and to contemplate. It means to think about what the Word has said and to ask yourself, "What does this mean to me? How do I apply it to my life?" It means to visualize God's Word working and becoming a reality in your life.

The Lord said to Joshua, This Book of the Law shall not depart from your mouth, but you shall meditate in it day and night, that you may observe to do according to all that is written in it. For then you will make your way prosperous, and then you will have good success (Joshua 1:8).

Ask for Direction Expecting to Hear from God

Instead of rushing headlong into a situation, we should first ask God what we are to do. The Word says that God hears our requests for His help and that He answers us, so we need to develop an attitude of expecting to hear from God.

David wrote, The steps of a good man are ordered by the LORD, and He delights in his way (Psalm 37:23).

And the Lord says to us, I will instruct you and teach you in the way you should go; I will guide you with My eye (Psalm 32:8).

Take Time to Listen and Hear God's Voice

Just as we must stop in the rush of life to hear what another has to say, we must stop and take time to listen to God. We can hear the voice of God through His Word, and also when He speaks to our spirits.

Isaiah wrote, Your ears shall hear a word behind you, saying, "This is the way, walk in it" (Isaiah 30:21).

Faith Comes by Hearing God's Word

Faith comes by hearing, and hearing the Word of God. True faith isn't based on what another person says. A person's testimony brings hope, but faith is based on knowing what God's Word says about our situation.

Abraham is our greatest example of faith. Not being weak in faith, he did not consider his own body, already dead (since he was about a hundred years old), and the deadness of Sarah's womb. He did not waver at the promise of God through unbelief, but was strengthened in faith, giving glory to God, and being fully convinced that what He had promised He was also able to perform (Romans 4:19–21).

Believe What God Has Spoken

What God has written in the Bible is for you, for me, for each individual. Take God's Word and apply it to your own situation. Meditate on a verse, and reword it to apply to yourself. For example, "Jesus said to me (Kathy or Joe or Alice), 'If you can believe, all things are possible to you when you believe.'" (See Mark 9:23.)

Write Down What God Has Spoken

When we take time to write down what God has said through His Word or personally to us, and how it applies to us, it makes that word more a part of our being.

The prophet Habakkuk wrote, Then the LORD answered me and said: "Write the vision and make it plain on tablets, that he may run who reads it" (Habakkuk 2:2).

Boldly Declare What God Has Spoken

When faith comes, it speaks. It tells others. Faith doesn't keep quiet "in case it doesn't work."

Paul wrote about faith speaking, But the righteousness of faith speaks in this way...But what does it say? "The word is near you, in your mouth and in your heart" (that is, the word of faith which we preach): that if you confess with your mouth the Lord Jesus and believe in your heart that God has raised Him from the dead, you will be saved. For with the heart one believes unto righteousness, and with the mouth confession is made unto salvation. (Romans 10:5, 8–10).

Obey! Act! Do It!

We read in Deuteronomy, It is not in heaven, that you should say, "Who will ascend into heaven for us and bring it to us, that we may hear it and do it?"

Nor is it beyond the sea, that you should say, "Who will go over the sea for us and bring it to us, that we may hear it and do it?"

But the word is very near you, in your mouth and in your heart, that you may do it (Deuteronomy 30:12–14).

Then Samuel said: "Has the LORD as great delight in burnt offerings and sacrifices, as in obeying the voice of the LORD? Behold, to obey is better than sacrifice, and to heed than the fat of rams. For rebellion is as the sin of witchcraft, and stubbornness is as iniquity and idolatry" (1 Samuel 15:22–23).

Have Patience

Most of the situations we have gotten ourselves into didn't happen in a moment of time, and they may take time to change. Many times, this is because it takes *us* time to change. If we were to receive an instant answer, we might do the same thing again. He will use the situation to change us before He changes the situation.

God has spoken to us often through the following Scriptures. Wait on the LORD; be of good courage, and He shall strengthen your heart; wait, I say, on the LORD! (Psalm 27:14).

Therefore do not cast away your confidence, which has great reward. For you have need of endurance, so that after you have done the will of God, you may receive the promise: "For yet a little while, and He who is coming will come and will not tarry (Hebrews 10:35–37).

Give Thanks

We should start giving thanks to the Lord at all times, not just when we see miracles. Giving thanks before the answer comes is an act of faith. It helps us to see how small our problems are in light of who God is.

The Psalms are full of praise. It is good to give thanks to the LORD, and to sing praises to Your name, O Most High (Psalm

92:1). Oh, give thanks to the LORD, for He is good! For His mercy endures forever....Oh, that men would give thanks to the LORD for His goodness, and for His wonderful works to the children of men! (Psalm 107:1, 8).

Your Miracle Will Come!

The Bible makes it so simple. All that is evil comes from Satan. All that is good comes from God. That's what Jesus said.

The thief [the Devil] does not come except to steal, and to kill, and to destroy. I [Jesus] have come that they may have life, and that they may have it more abundantly (John 10:10).

God desires only the best for us! In His redemptive work, Jesus has already provided every miracle we need in our lives. The apostle Paul wrote, Blessed be the God and Father of our Lord Jesus Christ, who has blessed us with every spiritual blessing in the heavenly places in Christ (Ephesians 1:3).

God wants to bless us with miracles more than we want to be blessed. In fact, He has already blessed us with every spiritual blessing.

CHAPTER ELEVEN

Supernatural Guidance

CHAPTER ELEVEN

Supernatural Guidance

The Bombs Exploded

A.L. was making flight plans for a ministry trip to Asia. He was talking over different flight options with me and said, "If I fly though India, it will take almost a day more, but we can save several hundred dollars."

I replied, "Don't save the money."

Don't save the money? Are you kidding? We always take the less expensive route. My instant answer was so totally unlike my usual thinking that it shocked us both. We started laughing and A.L. said with wonder, "I think we just heard from God. I'm not going to save the money." And he booked his tickets in a different direction.

The day A.L. would have been in the International Airport Terminal in Madras, India, terrorists bombed the airport, and many people were killed and injured!

That's not the only terrorist act God has saved us from. Once, we checked out of a hotel in Manila, and the next day the restaurant on the first floor was destroyed by a bomb. For three days, our friends and we had been in that restaurant having breakfast at that exact time.

Wow! What a mighty God we serve!

*H*ow are we to know what we are to do, where we are to go, who we are to talk to? We all need to listen for God's step-by-step directions for our lives.

There was a lady in Orange Country, California, who prayed in the morning and then started about her usual day. Usual for her, but not for most of us! "Okay, Lord," she would say, "I'm ready. Tell me who You want me to witness to today."

As she drove down the road, she would listen for God to speak. "Turn here," He would say. "Stop at that house." And she would do it. She would walk boldly up to the door, knock, and when the person who lived there answered the door, she would say something like, "God just told me to stop here and pray for you." Miracles happened. People accepted Jesus as their Lord and Savior. It wasn't unusual for her to come to church on Sunday morning with as many as fifteen new believers.

Our friend Nancy lives in the Northwest. She and her husband had spent an evening together with another couple, and as they were parting, someone suggested that they pray together. "I was so embarrassed," she said. "They were ready to leave, and I began to speak in tongues. I closed my eyes and went on and on speaking in another language. It was like I couldn't stop.

"My mind was arguing with what was happening. 'Lord, it's late. They're waiting to go home.' But the message continued on and on. I don't know how long I spoke. It was maybe as long as thirty minutes.

"Then, suddenly, it just stopped. I opened my eyes, and no one was with me. I turned around, and they were sitting at the table, writing on every scrap of paper they had been able to find.

"'Wow," they said in wonder, "you just gave us the entire itinerary for our trip. You have been speaking in Russian, and you have given us the dates we are to be in various cities. The names of the people we are to contact. Everything! And God finished by telling us that this would be the last trip we would be able to make into Russia, because we were getting much too well known to continue smuggling Bibles into that country.'"

That is an awesome example of supernatural guidance. But God is not always that definite.

Waiting on God's Leading

In 1968, when God had just healed A.L., our lives were still a mess. We didn't know what we were to do. In Houston, we had operated a Christian bookstore, but we both knew we couldn't go back. Going home would be like going back and facing death and defeat. And yet, we still had a family to support and house payments to make.

We had a personal friend who lived in the Los Angeles area, and A.L. set a time to get together with him. Before A.L. left for the meeting, we prayed that God would give us leading through this conversation, and we waited anxiously to hear what would be said.

When A.L. came home, he said, "He didn't give me any advice! He did suggest I might want to talk to a couple who have a chain of Christian bookstores, since we're in the same business and have been thinking of starting a chain store operation in Texas."

We had asked the Lord for guidance in that conversation, and so we followed the slight suggestion that was made. The next day, we met with the couple, and they asked us if we would be interested in managing one of their book-stores. We didn't know if we should be. What was God saying? All we knew was that we needed to look into it.

Our store in Houston was located in a shopping center. It had beautiful red carpet, white walls, and cherry wood fixtures. As you walked toward it, you could see that the aisles were wide. The store was neat, beautiful, and clean. The store's appearance drew the customers in.

In contrast, when we walked up to the store they had offered us, the windows were so dirty you couldn't see through them. When we went through the door, the interior was dingy and dark. Merchandise was literally hanging from the ceiling. The aisles were so narrow that you had to turn sideways to get through them. Books were stacked two and three rows deep. To get into the music section, you had to duck down into a tiny room where there was one light-bulb hanging from the ceiling. But when we walked about three feet into that store, a mantle of peace descended on both of us. It felt like we were wrapped in a warm, cozy blanket that we couldn't see.

In the natural, we never could have reasoned out the right choice of moving from what we had to what we were being offered, but God led us supernaturally, and we made the change.

We took our knowledge of what a Christian bookstore could be and changed that store. We worked twelve- and fourteen-hour days, six days a week. We cleaned, organized, built new fixtures, added light, and painted. That year, the sales were double what they had been the previous year. And in less than two years, A.L. was promoted to being the general manager over twenty-one stores.

God's guidance in this situation came to us in the form of a slight suggestion from a friend. And then, when we obediently followed that, God was more definite in His leading.

God's Vacation Plans

Several years later, we were thinking about buying a vacation home in the mountains. With so many managers reporting to A.L., our telephone rang day and night. We needed a place to be alone with our children, a place to get a little rest. As we looked and looked, working with various realtors, the cost of the homes we were looking at went up and up. Did God want us to have a vacation house, or was it just a desire of ours?

Finally, one evening, we prayed about it and made some definite decisions. We would pay a certain price, no more. We had so much for a down payment, no more. And we could afford a monthly payment of a certain amount, no more.

The next morning when we were leaving for the office, I told our son, John, who was taking care of our daughters that summer, "Stay around the house today. We may be going to Big Bear."

A.L. looked over at me. "Joyce," he said, "I think we have a lot of work to do at the office."

I laughed. "Boy, are you right! But John, stay close to the house today."

The morning flew by, and we went to lunch. When we walked back into the office, I said to A.L.'s secretary, "If a collect call comes in from Monty (a realtor we were working with then), accept the call." A.L. shook his head and walked on into his office even as the telephone started ringing.

It was Monty. "You won't believe the house that has just come on the market," he told A.L.

As he described it, A.L. knew the price must be way beyond what we had decided the night before. Finally, he asked, "Monty, how much is this house?"

"That's what you really won't believe," Monty replied. "It's listed at much less than its market value." The amount was what we had set the night before, to the penny.

"Ah, how much would they need for the down payment?" Again, it was the amount we had set, to the penny.

"Monty, what would our monthly payments be?" Again, right to the penny.

By the time he was off the phone, I had my desk cleared, my purse in my hand, and had asked our secretary to call John and tell him and our daughters to get ready. We were going to Big Bear. It took about two hours to pick up our family and make the drive, and we were as excited as children on Christmas morning. I remember saying, "A.L., we have to keep our feet on the ground and be sure this is what God is saying before we buy the house." I was concerned that our excitement would make us vulnerable.

The house Monty took us to was large. A window was broken; the interior wasn't completely finished, and it was filthy. But when we walked a few feet into the living room, peace descended on us. And I turned to Monty and said, "We'll take it!"

"But, but, but," he sputtered a bit and asked, "don't you want to see it first?" A.L. was laughing at what I'd said, after I had spent so much time on our drive up warning him that we shouldn't do that. But we both knew this was our house. And that vacation home, purchased in 1972, is our permanent home today.

Miracles seem so easy when we tell about them. It's hard for us to convey the time of turmoil and of prayer that has often gone on before the answer came. The time when we were desperately waiting for God to speak, yet not hearing a thing was the time that God used to develop our "faith muscles."

Walk in Confidence
That You Can Hear God's Voice

God doesn't want His people to be in bondage. We don't need to anxiously ask Him what to do at every turn in the road. Instead, we should walk in confidence, in faith, that He will tell us what is important, believing that we can hear His voice.

In the Psalms, we read, The steps of a good man are ordered by the LORD, and He delights in his way (Psalm 37:23).

David prayed, Uphold my steps in Your paths, that my footsteps may not slip. I have called upon You, for You will hear me, O God (Psalm 17:5–6).

And in Proverbs, we find, Trust in the LORD with all your heart, and lean not on your own understanding; in all your ways acknowledge Him, and He shall direct your paths (Proverbs 3:5–6).

We must move ahead in faith and confidence that He will order our steps and direct our paths. We must not be paralyzed for fear that we might make the wrong decision. Instead, we must move, believing we will hear from God when we need to make a change.

It is impossible to steer a ship that is sitting motionless in the water. However, when it's moving under power, the slightest movement of the helm will change its course.

As a friend and I were driving down a freeway toward Los Angeles to a specialty store, we were discussing how to know the will of God. We both were in a time of transition in our lives and knew God was going to be making some changes. I said to her, "It's like I'm driving on this freeway and you're going to tell me how to get to the store. I don't slow down at every exit and ask if I get off there. I trust you to tell me."

Then I realized that I *didn't* know where I was going. I had been to the store several times, but A.L. had been the one doing the driving. I didn't know which exit to take, and that was before the days of cell phones. Laughing, I said, "I don't know which exit to take. Let's listen to the Lord, and let Him tell us where to go."

She looked at me as if I were crazy, and I felt a little crazy, but I drove several more miles down the freeway. When I saw a certain exit coming up, I heard the Lord say, "Take that one." I did. At the traffic light, the Lord said, "Turn right." I did. Two or three blocks later, the Lord said, "Turn left," and I did.

Then when we were right in front of a little convenience store, the Lord said, "Now, go in there and ask for directions." We weren't in a very good area of town, and I did question my hearing a bit when I looked at the shabby store, but I went in and asked for directions.

The man began to laugh. "I just took my wife there yesterday," he said, and he drew a map for me. I had just a few blocks to go, but the way the streets intersected was confusing.

Why didn't the Lord lead me all the way? Certainly He could have, but in looking back on that day, I think I would have had trouble staying in the Spirit and hearing Him clearly. Perhaps I would have been like Peter when he walked on the water, and then began to look around. I was out there, I was hearing from God, but...

Follow the Leading of the Holy Spirit

We know that the Spirit led Jesus into the wilderness to be tempted. And sometimes, God will take us into hard places. That is the time we need to know we are exactly where He wants us.

We have a wonderful example of the leading of God in the story of Paul going to Macedonia in Acts, chapter sixteen. *Now when they had gone through Phrygia and the region of Galatia, they were forbidden by the Holy Spirit to preach the word in Asia (Acts 16:6).*

They were forbidden by the Holy Spirit to preach the word in Asia! Don't you wonder why and how?

After they had come to Mysia, they tried to go into Bithynia, but the Spirit did not permit them (v. 7).

The Spirit would not permit them. Again, we would like to know more. They may have been getting a little frustrated by this time. Travel wasn't easy, and they didn't even know where they were going. They just knew where they couldn't go.

So passing by Mysia, they came down to Troas. And a vision appeared to Paul in the night. A man of Macedonia stood and pleaded with him, saying, "Come over to Macedonia and help us" (vv. 8–9).

Now, finally, they have direction. They have seen a vision, and they have heard a voice.

Now after he had seen the vision, immediately we sought to go to Macedonia, concluding that the Lord had called us to preach the gospel to them.

Therefore, sailing from Troas, we ran a straight course to Samothrace, and the next day came to Neapolis, and from there to Philippi, which is the foremost city of that part of Macedonia, a colony.

And we were staying in that city for some days (vv. 10–12).

Do you feel a little discontent in those words? Or perhaps we are feeling a little of how we would be reacting in a similar situation. "Okay, Lord, we thought this was where you wanted us, but a number of days have passed, and nothing's happening. We saw the vision. We heard the voice. We obeyed. Now what?"

And on the Sabbath day we went out of the city to the riverside, where prayer was customarily made; and we sat down and spoke to the women who met there (v. 13).

They did the possible; they went where they knew people would be and spoke to them, and God put together a divine connection.

Now a certain woman named Lydia heard us. She was a seller of purple from the city of Thyatira, who worshiped God. The Lord opened her heart to heed the things spoken by Paul. And when she and her household were baptized, she begged us, saying, "If you have judged me to be faithful to the Lord, come to my house and stay" (Acts 16:14–15).

Through Lydia, they had a place to stay and an entrance for ministry into the community.

Some friends of ours who were missionaries were in Asia years ago, and they wanted to go back to a village where they had been before. But the political situation had changed, and they would not be allowed to enter the country. There was even a strong possibility that they would be imprisoned if they did enter. Their missionary friends said, "Don't go! But if you must, go after dark when the checkpoint might be unmanned." They prayed and felt impressed to leave at once, and they arrived at the checkpoint at about two in the afternoon. Normally this was a busy time of day, but there was no one on duty, and they just drove on through!

Two days later, they were ready to leave the country, but now it was even more dangerous to cross the border since they weren't officially there. This time, God impressed on them to leave early in the morning. And once again, the checkpoint was unmanned, and they just drove out of that country.

Walking in Guidance Is
a Process of Hearing and Obeying

Walking in supernatural guidance is a process. It's hearing from God and obeying. But the answer isn't always instantaneous. Often, there are days, weeks, months, even years, between the vision and its fulfillment. If God gave us all the direction at once, we might be tempted to say, "Okay, God, I can take it from here." We would probably begin walking in faith, but we might soon turn to walking by sight.

Walking in supernatural guidance can only be done in faith — in a continuous obedience of growing faith.

Supernatural Power and Protection

CHAPTER TWELVE

Supernatural Power and Protection

I yelled, "Jesus!"

It was late at night, and we were driving home. There was very little traffic, and A.L. was following another car down the highway. Both cars were going about seventy miles an hour.

We had been listening to a tape on the power of the name of Jesus, and I was meditating on the words we had just heard. Words like, **The name of the LORD is a strong tower; the righteous run to it and are safe (Proverbs 18:10).**

Could it be that if we just said the name Jesus, it was a complete prayer? When we exclaim, "Jesus," in faith, are we actually saying, "God save us"?

As I was drifting between meditating and sleeping, I heard A.L. gasp. My eyes flew open to see a police car racing down a road that intersected with ours. His lights were flashing. His siren was wailing. But there was no time for the car in front of us to stop, or even to slow enough for the police car not to hit it. There was going to be a terrible accident! And there was no way A.L. could avoid piling our car right into theirs. In the natural, there was no way out.

I wasn't even sure if I was awake or asleep, but I did exactly what I had been thinking about. My hand flew up and I pointed at the police car coming at us. "Jesus!" I yelled.

At that second, the police car was suddenly going down the road in the same direction we were going. He didn't swerve in a quick turn. He was instantly traveling in a different direction.

*W*hat a storm it must have been on the day Jesus calmed the sea! Mark wrote, And a great windstorm arose, and the waves beat into the boat, so that it was already filling. But He [Jesus] was in the stern, asleep on a pillow. And they awoke Him and said to Him, "Teacher, do You not care that we are perishing?"

Then He arose and rebuked the wind, and said to the sea, "Peace, be still!" And the wind ceased and there was a great calm (Mark 4:37–39).

How could Jesus speak to a storm and have it obey Him? Perhaps He did this one miracle in His power as God. Perhaps, just for a short time, He took back His rights and privileges as God. But that doesn't agree with what is written. Remember how we read that Jesus made Himself of no reputation, taking the form of a servant and coming in the likeness of men?

Remember how He laid aside His rights and privileges as God so that He could come to earth to live and die as a human being? *How* He did this is beyond our limited human understanding, but *that* He did it is not. Everything Jesus did on this earth He did as the Last Adam, as the man Adam was created to be.

When God created mankind, He gave them dominion on this earth. It is recorded in John that it was not because

Jesus was the Son of God that He was given authority on earth; He was given authority because He was the Son of Man. For as the Father has life in Himself, so He has granted the Son to have life in Himself, and has given Him authority to execute judgment also, because He is the Son of Man (John 5:26–27).

It's so important to understand that everything Jesus did on earth, He did as a man. That means – just like He said – "We can do it, too!"

Referring back to the storm, we see that Jesus chided the disciples even in the midst of this miracle of calming the elements. He said to them, "Why are you fearful, O you of little faith?" Then He arose and rebuked the winds and the sea, and there was a great calm (Matthew 8:26).

What didn't they have faith in? They knew Jesus could protect them. When they became afraid, they did the right thing. They came to Jesus. Was Jesus rebuking them for not having faith in God's power to protect them?

God Has Given Mankind Authority over the Earth

A.L. and I have written two books on the authority God has given to mankind. The following is a brief summary of this subject.

When God created Adam and Eve, He gave them authority over all the earth and everything that was in, or on, the earth. Adam and Eve surrendered that authority to Satan when they sinned, but Jesus came to take it back. He lived every day, moment by moment, by the laws He had set for Adam and Eve, so that He could, by His death, be our Substitute, our Redeemer, and take the keys of authority back from Satan.

These are the same keys of authority Jesus said He would give His church today.

Accounts of Supernatural Protection in the Bible

The Bible gives us many accounts of supernatural protection. God protected Noah, his family, and all the animals during the great judgment on all the earth.

When the children of Israel were at the shore of the Red Sea, God sent the pillar of fire and cloud between them and the Egyptians. It provided light for the Israelites, but was darkness to the Egyptians.

So it came between the camp of the Egyptians and the camp of Israel. Thus it was a cloud and darkness to the one, and it gave light by night to the other, so that the one did not come near the other all that night (Exodus 14:20).

And consider the fact that it was a cloud by day, protecting them from the heat of the desert, and a fire by night, providing warmth.

There were five kings of the Amorites who came up against Gibeon, and the Bible says that the Lord routed them and that He cast down large hailstones as they tried to flee, and they died.

When a great multitude, consisting of the armies of three nations, came against Judah and Jehoshaphat, God sent confusion on them, and they utterly destroyed each other.

God's Supernatural Protection Is for Today's Believers, Too

God's supernatural protection was not just for the children of Israel during the time of the Old Testament. It is for us today. Remember the storm that veered suddenly to the north in San Diego? That was not our first experience in moving in authority over the elements of our earth to bring protection.

Especially when we are speaking in authority, we must hear from God first. He must give us permission and instructions to move in this area.

Jesus said, I can of Myself do nothing. As I hear, I judge; and My judgment is righteous, because I do not seek My own will but the will of the Father who sent Me (John 5:30).

We must be careful not to try operating in authority to fulfill our own wills, our own desires. We must be doing the will of the Father, just as Jesus did.

Then Jesus said to them, When you lift up the Son of Man, then you will know that I am He, and that I do nothing of Myself; but as My Father taught Me, I speak these things (John 8:28).

In the seventies, California was experiencing a time of drought. Water was rationed, and our lakes were drying up. We flew over some of them, and they were just dry, cracked mud with a little water in the center. The situation was getting desperate.

We don't know how many times we asked the Lord, "Can we pray for rain?" Every time, we heard, "No, not yet." That answer was encouraging, because it meant the time was coming when we could pray, and we were persistent in asking permission.

Then one Sunday morning, God answered, "Today, you can pray for rain."

A.L. shared this with our pastor, and he said, "That confirms what God said to me." That morning, the whole church stood and asked God for rain, and on Tuesday, we had the first of several heavy rains, and that was the beginning of the end of the drought.

Just before the rains came, the hillsides were so dry in Southern California that any spark could set them on fire. The grass was so high that, when it burned, the heads of the grass would become firebombs driven by the wind over the fire lines. You have probably seen some of these horrible fires on the television news over the past years.

We were involved in the leadership of a ranch for abused children located in a picturesque canyon surrounded by meadows and trees. It was a wonderful, restoring atmosphere for children who had been so battered.

As I came out of the dry cleaners with our dry cleaning in one hand and my purse and car keys in the other, I looked up at the hillside above this ranch, and it was on fire. I knew instantly exactly what Satan's plan was. It was to burn this home and the surrounding buildings to the ground.

Somehow, I got everything in one hand, and with the other, I pointed at that fire. "Oh, no, you don't, Satan! In the name of Jesus, I command this fire to go out! In the name of Jesus, I say, you cannot continue burning!"

I didn't plan my words. I didn't think about what I was going to do. I saw the fire and knew what Satan planned. I don't remember transferring the things I was carrying from one hand to the other. I simply pointed at the fire, and the words came out.

David wrote, I am the LORD your God, who brought you out of the land of Egypt; open your mouth wide, and I will fill it (Psalm 81:10).

That's what happened to me that day. I was standing in the middle of the parking lot, but I wasn't conscious of the cars around me until I had spoken those words. Almost in shock, I got into the car and drove home, wondering what had happened. The next morning, the headlines of the newspaper reported, "Fire in Anaheim Hills Mysteriously Quits Burning!" The article speculated about how this could have happened, but the firemen had no answer. With hundreds of men fighting this fire, it still had been out of control, and then, they said, "The fire mysteriously quit burning."

The Believer's Authority

A.L. was teaching on the authority of the believer in a large church in Texas one Sunday morning. Every day, the news carried stories of a huge oil slick that was traveling across the Gulf of Mexico to the beaches of Texas. Every day, they painted a picture of the devastation that was coming to our beaches. But this Sunday morning, A.L. stopped teaching and talked to the class about the oil slick.

"We have authority," he said, "to stop this oil slick from coming on our coasts. Everyone who can believe with me, stand and extend your hands toward the Gulf." Most of the people stood, and A.L. took authority over that oil slick. I remember how he paused, searching for the right word in his spirit. "Dissipate," he said. "I command this oil slick to dissipate in the name of Jesus."

By now, you know the rest of the story. The newspapers reported, "Oil Slick Mysteriously Dissipates." The scientists couldn't explain it. It just disappeared.

The news media made fun of Pat Robertson several years ago when he said that he, or several people praying together, had stopped a hurricane from coming into Virginia Beach. We believe it! It sounds just like our God.

Years before, the staff of Campus Crusade, headquartered at that time in Southern California, took authority over a horrible forest fire that was raging toward their property. They said, "In the name of Jesus, you cannot touch our property." Right at their fence line, but not touching the fence, the wind reversed, and the fire went in another direction.

A friend of ours had been to A.L.'s seminar on the *Authority of the Believer*, and she called to tell us about standing on her porch in a flood situation and commanding the water to stop rising. She watched while the water stayed "piled up" in the center of the road. The neighbor across the street from her came over the next day and said, "Boy, am I glad we live across the street from you! I know you stopped the water from coming any higher!"

Another friend in Southern California told us about a fire burning up the hillside toward their home. She had heard our testimony of the fire that went out, and she stood by her house and took authority over that fire. "Fire, in the name of Jesus, you cannot burn our property." The fire kept coming, but she stood her ground. "Fire, I command you in the name of Jesus, you cannot burn our property!" The fire kept coming, but she continued to stand her ground, getting more and more certain of her faith. Finally, just when the fire reached the edges of their property, the wind turned, taking it in another direction.

One day, A.L. was driving our family down a rain-slick road, heading for church. We heard the loud squealing of brakes. It was a car sliding out of control. It crossed the center lane, and was coming right at us. "Jesus!" we cried, and the car hit what looked like a gold, but transparent, cowcatcher on the front of our car and slid, unharmed, back into its own lane.

We were sitting in the service when, all of a sudden, I realized, "There's no cowcatcher on the front of our car!" I had seen it there in the Spirit, and it had been so real that I didn't even think about it not being a part of our car until an hour or so later.

If you're of the younger generation and don't know what a cowcatcher is, it's the metal grille or frame that projected from the front of the old steam locomotives, and served to clear the track of obstructions.

Once, I was driving down the center lane on a freeway in Houston, Texas, and I heard a loud bang. Someone's tire had a blowout, I thought. But when I pulled ahead of the other cars, I realized that the flapping sound I was hearing was from *my* tire. I signaled to move right, drove off the freeway, and parked my car at the curb. I got out and walked to the rear of the car just in time to see the tire go flat.

It wasn't until years later, when I was listening to a lady tell about God protecting her that week when she had a blowout, that I realized what a miracle I had experienced.

After the service, I asked A.L., "What is the loud banging sound you hear when you have a blowout?"

"It's the air exploding out of the tire," he explained. Now I picture an angel flying alongside my car and holding it up until I changed lanes two times, drove normally off the freeway, and parked my car.

What Wonders Can Occur

God worked wondrous miracles of protection for His people throughout the Bible, and He is still working them for people today. We have just shared with you some of the miracles of protection and power that we know about. If we were sitting together around the table, we are sure you would be sharing with us similar miracles from your own experiences.

Oh, what wonders can occur when believers stop saying, "I can't," and start saying, "In the name of Jesus, I can. I can do the works of Jesus. I can live in the supernatural!"

CHAPTER THIRTEEN

Supernatural Provision

CHAPTER THIRTEEN

Supernatural Provision

A Supernatural Feast

Some close friends of ours were ministering to Indians in New Mexico. They lived near the reservation in a small camping trailer.

One Thanksgiving, they invited the Indians to their place for dinner, assuming a dozen people might show up and that everyone would bring food and there would be plenty for all. Charlie had measured their tiny oven and bought a turkey that would just fit. He and Norma had fixed some dressing, potatoes, gravy, and corn. But, of course, they were cooking on a small camping stove in small pans, and the amounts they prepared were small.

The Indians came in response to their invitation, and they were surprised to see about eighty people. None of them brought food, and Norma and Charlie knew they were in trouble. They didn't have enough food! What could they do? There wasn't money to go and buy food. There wasn't even time to buy food, even if there had been money, and they had invited these people to come to Thanksgiving dinner.

Charlie said, "God, we need a miracle," and while he continued praying in the name of Jesus, he began slicing their small turkey. He filled cookie sheet after cookie sheet with turkey. Norma began filling bowl after bowl with potatoes, dressing, gravy, and corn.

Charlie and Norma were still in awe when they told us about this miracle. "The people were even folding the food into napkins and filling their pockets and purses, but we never ran out of any item!"

What an awesome God we serve!

*W*e all know the story about Jesus taking the loaves and fish provided by the little boy and feeding the multitude. This incident is so important that it is recorded in all four Gospels, and we have included Matthew's account here.

When it was evening, His disciples came to Him, saying, "This is a deserted place, and the hour is already late. Send the multitudes away, that they may go into the villages and buy themselves food."

But Jesus said to them, "They do not need to go away. You give them something to eat."

And they said to Him, "We have here only five loaves and two fish."

He said, "Bring them here to Me." Then He commanded the multitudes to sit down on the grass. And He took the five loaves and the two fish, and looking up to heaven, He blessed and broke and gave the loaves to the disciples; and the disciples gave to the multitudes.

So they all ate and were filled, and they took up twelve baskets full of the fragments that remained. Now those who had eaten were about five thousand men, besides women and children (Matthew 14:15–21).

Whenever we read an incident in the Bible, we ask ourselves, Why is it recorded? Why is it important to me? By choice, we're believers. We believe the Word of God is true, but beyond that, we have a hunger to understand why it is there for us to read. Our response has become, "Yes, this happened, but Lord, why is it important for us to know about it?"

Can believers today enter into supernatural provision? Is there a secret we need to understand for the time in which we live? Was this supernatural provision of food for the time of Jesus only? Was this a onetime supernatural intervention of God?

No, we read of Jesus feeding four thousand men, plus the women and children, with seven loaves and a few fish a short time later.

When Hagar and Ishmael were wandering in the Wilderness of Beersheba, their water was gone, and, in the natural, they had no hope. But they cried out to God, and we read, **Then God opened her eyes, and she saw a well of water. And she went and filled the skin with water, and gave the lad a drink (Genesis 21:19).**

We've already told you about the supernatural communion when God multiplied the bread, but we've experienced more miracles of provision in our lives.

When we received the baptism of the Holy Spirit, we were working for a Christian company, but they didn't believe in the baptism of the Holy Spirit. A.L. was teaching the adult Sunday school class in a church that didn't believe in the baptism of the Holy Spirit. Most of our friends were non-Pentecostal. And we were in for many changes in the next few months.

The Holy Spirit inspired the writers of the Bible, and in the months following our baptism, He wonderfully began to open the Word of God to our understanding.

The Holy Spirit also told us of things that were going to happen, but we couldn't seem to understand them. We met over breakfast with a prophet of God, and he began to speak into our lives. He gave us the time frame in which these things would be happening. He used the same verses God had given us and explained them. First, there would be three months of verbal assault, then three months of silence; then there would be three months of being without work before we found our new way.

Three months without work! Even in our worst financial crises, we had always had work! How would we live? We had three children, a car, two houses, and bills! What were we to do? We didn't understand faith, beyond faith for salvation. We hadn't even heard much about it. During the first six months, we saved about one-third of everything that came in. We were diligent in preparation for what lay ahead.

We wish we could tell you of our marvelous faith during this time. How we walked in peace through these months; but we can't, because we didn't. Our faith was very up-and-down. But we can tell you about the wonderful presence of God we felt when we were asked to leave our church, when our friends suddenly didn't seem to know us, and when we were fired from the Christian company where we worked. During this time, God was showing us His presence in supernatural ways.

For years, we had instant protein for breakfast. Each day, I dumped five scoops of protein powder into the blender, along with milk and seasoning. A two-pound can of protein lasted less then a month.

It wasn't my habit to look into the can each morning. I pulled it forward on the shelf, which was a little above my eyesight, scooped out the protein I needed, and pushed it back into place. For three months, I took out five scoops of protein each morning, and the can never went down in content. The morning A.L. joined the staff of a large charismatic church in Southern California, I reached into the can of protein with my scoop, and my hand went all the way to the bottom of the can. I picked it up, turned it over, and was able to shake just enough protein for that day into the blender.

We enjoyed God's supernatural provision during this hard time. We praised Him continuously for being with us.

Also, we drove a Buick sedan, and we knew from experience that we could drive to our place in the mountains, around the lake one time, and home on one tank of gas. For three months, we made the same trip and used half a tank of gas. Our gasoline mileage doubled.

During this time, we made a trip from Whittier to Sacramento, California, to join some friends for a time of ministry. As we left home, we thanked the Lord for what he had done to multiply our gasoline and asked Him to continue stretching our mileage. We drove there on one tank of gasoline, when normally it would have taken at least two.

We weren't destitute. We had money in savings. We could have purchased these items, but God was showing us that He has supernatural provision for His people.

The Great Multiplier

I was pondering this time of multiplication a few years ago, and I asked the Lord once again to show me His supernatural provision. We used a special healthy sweetener, and I felt we were paying way too much for it. I thanked the Lord for multiplying that sweetener each time I used it. And we used the same little container month after month until the plastic wore out and collapsed in my hand!

We were sharing some of these miracles with a worship leader, and he shared with us about his childhood. His mom was a single mother with several children, and many times there was no money for food. They would go all day with one meal, or even no meal. But each night, before they went to bed, his family gathered together and began to sing praises to the Lord. He said, "We never went to bed hungry. Each night, when we praised and worshipped the Lord, God would fill our stomachs, and we went to bed full!"

Let's read the words of David and listen to the heart-cry of God. I am the LORD your God, who brought you out of the land of Egypt; open your mouth wide, and I will fill it....

Oh, that My people would listen to Me, that Israel would walk in My ways! I would soon subdue their enemies, and turn My hand against their adversaries....

He would have fed them also with the finest of wheat; and with honey from the rock I would have satisfied you (Psalm 81:10, 13–14, 16).

We tell about miracles in order to raise our faith level. Remembering what God has done encourages us. Knowing what God has done for us and others should encourage you. God is no respecter of persons (Acts 10:34 KJV). That means He doesn't show partiality to one person over another. What He has done for one person, He will do for another who believes.

Supernatural Provision in the Bible

Supernatural provision is not a one- or two-time deal in Scripture. There is an account in 2 Kings that we overlooked for many years.

Then a man came from Baal Shalisha, and brought the man of God bread of the firstfruits, twenty loaves of barley bread, and newly ripened grain in his knapsack. And he said, "Give it to the people, that they may eat."

But his servant said, "What? Shall I set this before one hundred men?"

He said again, "Give it to the people, that they may eat; for thus says the LORD: 'They shall eat and have some left over.'"

So he set it before them; and they ate and had some left over, according to the word of the LORD (2 Kings 4:42–44).

In addition, the ravens fed Elijah, and then the widow fed him. Let's read that account.

Then the word of the LORD came to [Elijah], saying, "Arise, go to Zarephath, which belongs to Sidon, and dwell there. See, I have commanded a widow there to provide for you."

So he arose and went to Zarephath. And when he came to the gate of the city, indeed a widow was there gathering sticks. And he called to her and said, "Please bring me a little water in a cup, that I may drink." And as she was going to get it, he called to her and said, "Please bring me a morsel of bread in your hand."

So she said, "As the LORD your God lives, I do not have bread, only a handful of flour in a bin, and a little oil in a jar; and see, I am gathering a couple of sticks that I may go in and prepare it for myself and my son, that we may eat it, and die."

And Elijah said to her, "Do not fear; go and do as you have said, but make me a small cake from it first, and bring it to me; and afterward make some for yourself and your son. For thus says the LORD God of Israel: 'The bin of flour shall not be used up, nor shall the jar of oil run dry, until the day the LORD sends rain on the earth.'"

So she went away and did according to the word of Elijah; and she and he and her household ate for many days. The bin of flour was not used up, nor did the jar of oil run dry, according to the word of the LORD which He spoke by Elijah (1 Kings 17:9–16).

What a miracle of provision this was! Elijah was sent to a widow, a widow with a son, and he said, "First you feed me, and then God will multiply your food."

She didn't know God. Notice that she said, "The Lord *your* God." Elijah could have been tricking her out of the last of her food, but in believing and giving, she received.

Moreover, for the children of Israel, God sent manna. He sent quail. He provided water in the desert.

The Secret Is in the Sharing

In our special communion, when we broke bread together, the bread was multiplied. It was far more than enough. When Jesus fed the multitude, He broke the loaves, and they were multiplied. It seems that the secret of supernatural provision is often in the sharing.

So often we think of God's promise in Luke as pertaining to money, but Jesus said, **Give, and it will be given to you: good measure, pressed down, shaken together, and running over will be put into your bosom. For with the same measure that you use, it will be measured back to you (Luke 6:38).**

We wonder if Joseph was actually able to store enough food for the whole world for seven years, or if, because he was obedient and did what God instructed, God brought the increase.

Another area of contemplation concerns Noah and the ark. Was Noah able to store enough food for all the animals for the length of time they were in the ark? Or did God provide substance supernaturally?

Let Your Faith Be Stretched

We challenge you. Step out now in this area of faith. Believe God for supernatural provision for something small today, and let your faith be stretched and ready for whatever may lie ahead.

CHAPTER FOURTEEN

Miracles Are Still Happening

Miracles Are Still Happening!

The Clouds Divided

A.L. had taken a group of people to Israel, and one night he was praying concerning the time he would be speaking to them. The Lord showed Him the Holy Spirit coming on the group and many of them receiving the baptism in the Holy Spirit. They would be in the ancient Roman coliseum in Caesarea. That was the city where Peter came to the house of Cornelius and the Holy Spirit fell, for the first time, on the Gentiles.

The next day, they went to the coliseum. It was a beautiful setting, and the group was looking out over the Mediterranean Sea. As A.L. spoke, they could see a terrible storm coming up behind him. The other tour groups were running for their buses, but A.L. continued teaching. He knew what God had shown him, and he wasn't moved by what was happening around him. The people stayed with him. If he wasn't running, they weren't either. But it got darker and darker, and the storm became even more threatening.

Then A.L. said, "The Holy Spirit is going to fall on you in power!" He raised both hands into the air exactly as he had seen himself doing the night before. And when he did, the Holy Spirit fell, and everyone began to speak in other tongues, including many who at that moment received the baptism in the Holy Spirit.

Also, at the same instant in which he raised his hands, the clouds divided right above them and fled in two directions. In a matter of seconds, there was a beautiful blue sky overhead.

For the rest of their tour, their Jewish guide said, over and over, "I can't believe it! The clouds just parted!"

*W*riting *Miracles Are Still Happening* has been a special endeavor for us. We have enjoyed going back over the years and thinking about the wonderful things God has done. We haven't written about the days and nights of grieving over lost dreams that we have gone through – the times of questioning God – the times we have felt lost in the middle of the ocean – the defeats that seemed to suffocate us. The reason is simple. Over the years, those times have become less and less important to us. They have become harder and harder to remember. They have been worth the changes God has brought about in our lives.

We have made this a life-long habit: **Forgetting those things which are behind and reaching forward to those things which are ahead, [we] press toward the goal for the prize of the upward call of God in Christ Jesus (Philippians 3:13–14).**

Any Miracle in the Bible Can Happen to You Today

Our desire in writing this book has been to encourage you to step into the miraculous. We firmly believe that any miracle found in the Bible can happen in any believer's life today. God never changes! He may be calling someone to be a Moses to his family, or to his people. He may be calling someone to be a John the Baptist, crying in the wilderness,

"Repent!" He may be calling someone to be an evangelist like Philip, or a martyr like Stephen. He may be calling someone to be a modern-day apostle like Paul.

But we know, beyond any doubt, that He is calling believers, as they go about their normal days, to say, "**The kingdom of heaven is at hand**" (Matthew 10:7). He is calling every believer to move in the wonderful gifts of the Spirit – to heal the sick, cleanse the lepers, raise the dead, and cast out demons. He is calling every believer to do the works of Jesus.

Our pasts have been forgiven. The Son of God has commissioned us. We have been empowered by the Holy Spirit. It's time we raised our heads, threw off the shackles of our old lives, and said with Jesus, **The Spirit of the LORD is upon Me, because He has anointed Me to preach** [to bring the good news of] **the gospel to the poor; He has sent Me to heal the brokenhearted, to proclaim** [to bring the good news of] **liberty to the captives and recovery of sight to the blind, to set at liberty those who are oppressed** (Luke 4:18).

In reading about one miracle after another, as you have done in this book, you may have begun to think, "Greater is He that's in Joyce and A.L. than He that's in me," but that's not true!

God gave us wonderful encouragement when John was inspired to write these words of Jesus: **You are of God, little children, and have overcome them, because He who is in you is greater than he who is in the world** (1 John 4:4).

You have been reading about miracles that have happened to us over more than thirty years. The only reason we have shared them is to encourage you to step into a supernatural way of living yourself.

Soon after we received the baptism in the Holy Spirit, we started attending a Prayer and Share meeting on Thursday mornings. We would hear testimony after testimony that challenged our faith. We've never forgotten one lady who told about seeing a terrible accident. She told how the truck driver was lying all crumpled up, some distance from his truck. The people around him said he was dead, but she asked them to make room for her. She knelt in the grass beside him and commanded him to live in the name of Jesus, and he did! She wasn't a pastor or an evangelist, and she certainly wasn't an "ordinary" believer. She was a supernatural, Spirit-filled believer who was at the right place at the right time. She was a believer operating in the supernatural gifts of the Holy Spirit.

Hearing testimonies of the supernatural were a great help to us when we were struggling to move from our natural way of living to the supernatural. We were with people who prayed for parking places, openings in traffic, promotions on the job, healing, finances, and new cars and trucks; and they shared with us the answers to their prayers. We learned to pray about everything, all the time. We prayed about where to eat, and even sometimes about what to wear. We got into the habit of talking to God just as though He was with us, and it worked! He is Immanuel — God with us!

Any Miracle Is a "Big" Miracle

There are no such things as big miracles and little miracles. Any miracle that happens to us is big. One missionary who has gone on to be with the Lord used to say, "I'm trying to think of something to ask God for that is so big He would have to move His little finger to accomplish it."

You could probably record miracle after miracle of the things that have happened to you — your miracles of protection, guidance, and provision.

For too long, many of us have felt intimidated by others. If we talk about the supernatural, what will people think? Will they think we're strange? Will they laugh at us?

People Are Looking for the Supernatural Power of God

When we look around us, we see people involved in New Age, the occult, séances, and witchcraft. We see people searching for answers in all the wrong places. They are looking for the supernatural power of God. We should have the answers. We should have the power of God flowing through us.

As we share our miracles with others, they will be encouraged to start seeking God in a new way. Others will be challenged to step into a supernatural way of living themselves.

Miracles Are Happening Today

One day, with our friends in the car with us, we left San Diego right at the peak of traffic. Our friends were speaking in Escondido, and we had been delayed at the Christian television station. We came over the overpass onto the center lane of the freeway, and when we did, we could see that the traffic ahead was moving very slowly. In the natural, we would never make it to the meeting on time. There were six of us in the car, and as we saw the situation, no one said a word in English. At the same instant, we all pointed to the traffic ahead and began to speak in tongues. We drove mile after mile at the speed limit, watching turn signals come on and every car in our lane move to the right, getting out of our way.

After several minutes of this miracle, we were coming to a small red sports car, and it didn't seem to be moving over. I said to A.L., in English, "How do you say 'little red sports car' in tongues?" It was as if he answered me, still speaking in tongues, and that car, also, quickly moved out of our way.

For forty minutes, A.L. drove without one time touching the brakes, and we were able to get our friends to their meeting on time.

I've always wondered what those drivers saw. Did we appear to them as an emergency vehicle with a flashing red light on top?

Sweet Memories

A.L. and I love to talk about the supernatural things of God. We get into the most interesting conversations with people that way. One memory triggers another, and one miracle after another pours out of "ordinary" believers, excited about sharing what God has done for them.

A pastor friend told us about a time she was driving an older car, and God told her not to drive the car up the last two steep blocks to her boys' school. But her boys had pleaded with her not to make them walk, and she had agreed to drive the first block, but not the second. As she started down the hill, her brakes went out. "God, forgive me for not listening to you!" were her first words.

Her emergency brakes didn't work. She turned the motor off, but even without power, her car was gaining more and more speed. She tried scraping the tires against the curb, but the car jumped the curb and she had to pull it back onto the street. The car blasted through a crosswalk. People were yelling at her. There were children on both sides of the road. "God," she cried out. "What can I do?"

"Turn right!" God said. There was a small street there, and she turned her car to the right into that street. Immediately, her car was stopped. She didn't hit anything. She didn't feel the force of the car suddenly stopping. The car was just stopped!

A man told us about a time when he was in seminary. He was driving a long distance to the church where he was ministering one Sunday morning. He was traveling about seventy miles an hour, when an eighteen-wheeler pulled out from a side street, right in front of him, blocking the road. He was so close to the truck that he was looking under it. There was no way he could stop in time. He told us how he cried out, "Jesus," because he thought he was going to die. But instantly, he was on the other side of the truck – looking at it in his rearview mirror. "Oh," he said, "I've never told anyone about this before. Who would believe me?"

Exciting things are happening as we drive our cars! But praise God, He is just as active in the rest of our lives.

Some friends of ours were in a refugee camp in Thailand when a two-year-old girl drowned in a baptismal pool. The father was holding her upside down by one foot and slapping her on the back, but nothing was happening. She was dead. She had turned blue, and there was no pulse or heartbeat. Our friends took her little body and rebuked the spirit of death. The Lord told one of our friends to blow into her mouth, and after five deep breaths, she began to move her arms, and her eyelids fluttered. After five more breaths, her eyeballs came back into place, and she began to cry. They were able to place her into her mother's arms! When they were back in the refugee camp six months later, they looked up this family, and the little girl was fine. There was no brain damage.

Another friend was on the beach in the Caribbean when there was a loud lamenting, and a large crowd began to gather. She ran over to see what had happened and found that young man had just drowned, and they had pulled his body out of the water. She knelt in the sand beside his body and commanded life to come back into it, and it did.

Betty and her sister were in the kitchen getting lunch when they heard a terrible scream from outside. Knowing that their husbands were working on their car, they ran to see what had happened. The car, a '56 Ford Fairlane, had fallen off the jack, and Betty's husband was trapped underneath. Her brother-in-law was trying to lift the car up, and they joined him, but nothing was happening. Betty yelled, "God, we've got to have some help!"

She writes, "The car just slowly went up. I went around and pulled Carl out from under it. Then, we all looked at our hands, and there were no marks of having done any kind of heavy lifting. God had just stepped in and lifted that car off Carl."

A friend in Houston, Texas, was walking into a dry cleaners when he heard God say, "Tell her that the God her mother prays to has sent you this morning." He was obedient. "The God your mother prays to has sent me to you," he said immediately. The young lady began to cry, and soon she was praying and getting right with God.

A doctor in Malaysia told us about a young boy dying in his clinic. This was a very dangerous thing to have happen, since the young boy was of a different religion and the doctor could have ended up in prison. The clinic would have been closed. There seemed to be no medical reason for the young man's death. He had just stopped breathing. "God," the doctor prayed, "You know what his death here can mean to me and this clinic. I ask You in the name of Jesus to bring this young man back to life." And immediately, he came back to life.

A couple from California took their vacation time each year and ministered in Mexico. They weren't ministers, and they didn't speak Spanish, but they ventured out by themselves, doing whatever the Spirit led them to do. One day, they came to a village, and the people motioned them into a small home. When they went in, they saw, and they smelled, an older lady who was lying on the bed, dead. It looked as if most of the people from the village were crowded into that room, mourning her passing.

They walked up to the bed and, standing beside the dead lady, began to speak in the Spirit. (Later, they realized they had been speaking in Spanish.) They spoke on and on, and suddenly the wife realized she had put her hand on the forehead of the dead woman's body – and the body was moving!

The lady's family came back to the village carrying her casket and found her alive. She walked through the village for three days, and everyone in that village came to Jesus! And then, she lay back down and died.

We didn't know this couple. A.L. overheard their story one day when he was eating in a restaurant. They had just come back to the States and were marveling about what God had done. Of course, A.L. introduced himself and asked for all the details.

Notice that only two of the miracles in this chapter happened to us. People are beginning to talk about the wondrous things they have seen God do. Miracles are happening everywhere in the world.

Jesus has appeared in mosques. He has appeared in counseling clinics. He has appeared in the clouds. He has appeared in the eyes of people reaching out to us in love.

"Just Do It!"

God is speaking to His church today, "Just do it!" So many of us have been waiting for the right time – the right education – the right position – the right financial situation – or the right group to believe with us. We have been talking about what we are going to do in the future. To all of us, God is saying, "Just do it! Start!"

A good friend, who has gone on to be with the Lord, used to say, "Do something, lest you do nothing!"

The secret of seeing miracles is, first, being born of the Spirit and coming into the family of God; second, being filled with His Holy Spirit and allowing the Spirit of God to flow through us in power; and third, walking in faith, in expectancy that God will work miracles on our behalf.

Jesus said, **He who believes in Me, as the Scripture has said, out of his heart will flow rivers of living water (John 7:38).**

Look for opportunities to pray. Listen to the news and to God at the same time. Let Him tell you how to pray in situations that have nothing to do with you, but are ones in which He wants you to get involved in the Spirit.

Read through the Gospels and the book of Acts again and again, taking time to visualize yourself doing exactly what Jesus and the apostles did. Picture yourself doing the works of Jesus. Imagine yourself working miracles. As you read each miracle, boldly declare, "If Jesus did it, I can do it, too."

Pray in the Spirit everywhere you go, expecting God to speak or to show you your next miracle. Then boldly do what He has told you to do. From this day forward, you can live a life where miracles are still happening!

Scripture References for Bible Miracles in

Miracles Are Still Happening

Note: This is not meant to be an exhaustive list of biblical miracles, but rather a convenient list of references to the specific miracles cited in this book, in the order in which they are mentioned. In some cases, only one reference is given for a miracle, even though it may be found in more than one place in the Scriptures. Most Scriptures already referenced within the text of the book are not repeated here.

Chapter One: Miracles, Miracles, Miracles

Creation..Genesis 1:1–2
The Flood..Genesis 6:1–9:1
Sarah Giving Birth to Isaac............................Genesis 17:15–19; 21:1–3
The Translation of Enoch................................Genesis 5:21–24
Miracles in the Life of Moses:
    Life preserved in basket on Nile ....Exodus 1:15–2:10
    Called through the burning bush ....Exodus 3:1–4:17
    Rod turning into a snake............................Exodus 7:10
    Plagues in Egypt..Exodus 7:14–12:36
    Parting of Red Sea....................................Exodus 14
    Supernatural water ....Exodus 17:1–6; Numbers 20:7–11
    Supernatural manna and quail ....Exodus 16:11–35
    Clothing and shoes not wearing out .... Deuteronomy 8:4
    Supernatural pillars of cloud and fire ....Exodus 13:21–22
    Ten Commandments written by finger of God ....Exodus 31:18
Miracles in the Life of Joshua:
    Parting of Jordan River...............................Joshua 3:7-17
    Commander of Lord's army appearing........Joshua 5:13–6:5
    Hail destroying armies at Gibeon ....Joshua 9:1–10:11
    Sun standing still......................................Joshua 1-:12–14
    Walls of Jericho falling down ....Joshua 6:12–20
Gideon and the Fleece....................................Judges 6:36–40

Miracles in Samson's Life and Death ....Judges 13:2–16:30
Dagon Falling before Ark of God ....1 Samuel 5:1–4
David Defeating Goliath..1 Samuel 17:4–51
Jonah Swallowed by and Kept Alive in Great Fish ....Jonah 1–2
Miracles in the Life of Hezekiah:
    Healed of fatal sickness... 2 Kings 20:1–7
    Shadow of sun going back ten degrees .... 2 Kings 20:8–11
Miracles in the Life of Elijah:
    Rain stopping and starting ....1 Kings 16:29–17:1; 18:1–45
    Fed by ravens .... 1 Kings 17:2–6
    Fed through multiplication of oil and flour................ 1 Kings 17:8–16
    Widow's son brought back to life ....1 Kings 17:17–24
    Fire falling from heaven ....1 Kings 18:17–39
    Parting of Jordan River... 2 Kings 2:8
    Translation to heaven.. 2 Kings 2:9–12
Miracles in the Life and Death of Elisha:
    Parting of Jordan River... 2 Kings 2:13–14
    Multiplication of oil for widow and sons .... 2 Kings 4:1–7
    Prophecy of birth of Shunammite's son .... 2 Kings 4:8–17
    Son brought back to life... 2 Kings 4:18–37
    Poisoned pottage made good to eat............................2 Kings 4:38–41
    Iron ax head made to float .... 2 Kings 6:1–7
    Healing of Naaman's leprosy .... 2 Kings 5:1–14
    Leprosy coming on Gehazi for his sin ....2 Kings 5:15–27
    Opening of blind eyes.. 2 Kings 6:8–23
    Bones bringing life to dead man..............................2 Kings 13:20–21

Chapter Two: Jesus Performed Miracles

Miracles surrounding Christ's Birth:
    Angel appearing to Mary..Luke 1:26–38
    Angel appearing to Joseph......................................Matthew 1:20–21
    Angels appearing to shepherds.......................................Luke 2:8–14
    Wise men guided to Jesus by star............................Matthew 2:1–11
    Wise men warned about Herod in dream......................Matthew 2:12
    Joseph warned to flee to Egypt in dream ....Matthew 2:13

Scripture References for Miracles in the Text

Jesus' Miracles of Healing:

Nobleman's son .... John 4:46–54

Leper .... Matthew 8:2–3

Paralytic let down through roof .... Mark 2:1–12

Infirm man at Pool of Bethesda .... John 5:2–9

Man with withered hand .... Luke 6:6–10

Woman with issue of blood .... Mark 5:25–34

Demon-possessed, blind, and mute man .... Matthew 12:22

Two blind men .... Matthew 9:27–31; 20:30–34

Blind man at Bethsaida .... Mark 8:22–25

Man born blind .... John 9:1–7

Bartimaeus, the blind beggar .... Mark 10:46–52

Centurion's servant .... Matthew 8:5–13

Syro-Phoenician woman's daughter .... Mark 7:24–30

Ten lepers .... Luke 17:12–19

Man with dropsy .... Luke 14:1–4

Ear of servant of high priest .... Luke 22:47–51; John 18:1–11

Incidents of Jesus healing all .... Matthew 12:15; Luke 4:40;
      Matthew 14:36; Mark 6:56; Luke 6:19; Matthew 15:30–31

Jesus' Miracles of Deliverance:

Demoniac in Capernaum synagogue .... Mark 1:21–27

Demoniac in region of Gadarenes .... Mark 5:1–17

Bent-over woman with spirit of infirmity .... Luke 13:10–17

Jesus' Miracles in Nature:

Water turned into wine at Cana wedding .... John 2:1–11

Feeding of five thousand .... John 6:5–14

Feeding of four thousand .... Mark 8:1–9

Miraculous amounts of fish caught .... Luke 5:1–11; John 21:1–11

Fish with tax money in mouth .... Matthew 17:24–27

Storm stilled .... Mark 4:35–41

Fig tree cursed .... Matthew 21:18–22

Walking on water .... John 6:16–21

Jesus' Miracles of Raising the Dead:

Jairus's daughter .... Mark 5:22–43

Widow of Nain's son .... Luke 7:11–17

Lazarus .... John 11:1–45

Chapter Four: The Dunamis Power

Chapter Six: The Church Begins in Power

Chapter Eight: Moving in the Supernatural

Chapter Nine: The Choice Is Ours

Scripture References for Miracles in the Text

Chapter Twelve: Supernatural Power–Protection

Chapter Thirteen: Supernatural Provision

About the Authors

A.L. AND JOYCE GILL are internationally known speakers, authors, and Bible teachers. A.L.'s apostolic ministry travels have taken him to over sixty nations of the world. He has preached in person to crowds exceeding one hundred thousand, and to many millions more by radio and television.

Their top-selling books and manuals have sold millions of copies in the United States. Their writings, which have been translated into many languages, are being used in Bible schools and seminars around the world.

The powerful, life-changing truths of God's Word explode in the lives of others through their dynamic preaching, teaching, writing, video and audio tape ministry.

The awesome glory of the presence of God is experienced in their praise and worship seminars as believers discover how to become true and intimate worshippers of God. Many have discovered a new and exciting dimension of victory and boldness through their teachings on the authority of the believer.

The Gills have trained many believers to step into their own God-given supernatural ministries with the healing power of God flowing through their hands. Many have learned to be "supernaturally natural" as they are released to operate in all nine gifts of the Holy Spirit in their daily lives and ministries.

Both A.L. and Joyce have Master of Theological Studies degrees. A.L. has also earned a Doctor of Philosophy in Theology degree from Vision International University. Their ministry is solidly based on the Word of God, centered on Jesus, strong in faith, and taught in the power of the Holy Spirit.

The Gills' ministry is a demonstration of the Father's heart of love. Their preaching and teaching are accompanied by powerful anointing, signs, wonders, and healing miracles, with many being slain in the Spirit in waves under the power of God.

Signs of revival and awesome manifestations of God's glory and power are being experienced by many who attend their meetings.

The Gills are available to minister at your church,
seminar, conference, or revival meetings. You can learn
more about their ministry through their website:
http://www.gillministries.com
You may contact them through their office at
Gill Ministries, PO Box 99, Fawnskin, CA 92333
E-mail: algill@bigbear.net